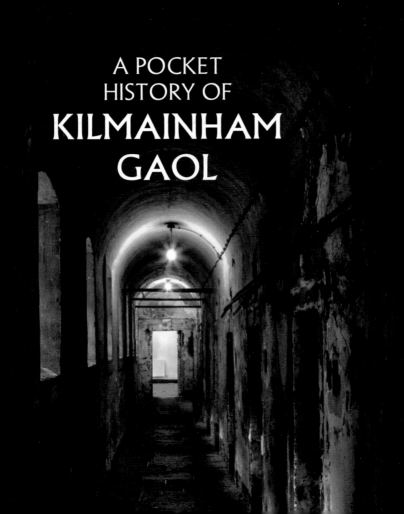

A POCKET
HISTORY OF
KILMAINHAM
GAOL

Gill Books
Hume Avenue, Park West, Dublin 12

www.gillbooks.ie

Gill Books is an imprint of M.H. Gill & Co.

Copyright © Teapot Press Ltd 2021

ISBN: 978-0-7171-8989-2

This book was created and produced by Teapot Press Ltd

Text by Richard Killeen
Edited by Fiona Biggs
Designed by Tony Potter
Picture research by Joe Potter & Tony Potter

The author is deeply grateful to Pat Cooke and Brian Crowley, who
reviewed the text, made many valuable corrections and suggestions
and saved him from a number of embarrassing errors. Any remaining
errors and omissions are entirely the author's.

Printed in Europe
This book is typeset in Dax and Minion Pro

5 4 3 2 1

A POCKET HISTORY OF
KILMAINHAM GAOL

Richard Killeen

Gill Books

Contents

Charles Stewart Parnell arrives at Kilmainham Gaol, in a scene depicted in *The Graphic*, 1881.

Charles Stewart Parnell and John Dillon in Kilmainham Gaol in a Vanity Fair print of 1881 entitled *Force No Remedy*.

Introduction

It seems like a silly question, but it isn't. Why are there prisons at all? There have always been places of incarceration, like the Tower of London, where traitors or suspected traitors were lodged. There is a clue in that formula. Originally, such places were reserved for enemies – or suspected enemies – of the state. The majority of ordinary crimes, such as murder, theft and so on, were not always regarded as any kind of threat to the state. Accordingly, the state very often ignored them, regarding them as essentially private matters, rather like civil as distinct from criminal matters in modern law.

The prevailing system in many parts of the world was what was called retributive justice. It's best summed up in the famous biblical formula of an eye for an eye and a tooth for a tooth. In other words, it was a private matter between victim and perpetrator – or their extended families. The state stayed out of it. We have all heard of the vendetta, the seemingly endless cycle of killing and counter-killing that can run down the generations in societies that we all too easily denominate as 'backward'. If someone from Family A kills someone from Family B, there then rests a moral responsibility on Family B to avenge their dead kinsman by killing someone from Family A, very often the eldest surviving son. That triggers a cycle, which can last in some cases for generations, until some sort of settlement is brokered, often by contracting a marriage between the two families.

I have stressed the word 'moral' in that passage, because that is how this obligation was – and in many societies today still is – felt. It was a matter of honour and duty. As for the state, it was none of its business. Murders, thefts and other such offences were essentially private matters between two aggrieved parties, or by extension two aggrieved families and their extended networks. So they were left to get on with it. Even today, this is how territorial wars between drugs gangs are settled. In the eyes of the gangs that prosecute these wars, they are strictly private business – nothing to do with the state or its institutions. We'll settle these things our own way, thank you very much.

This is indeed how gang culture everywhere operates, whether it is Chinese Triads, Los Angeles street gangs, or the Mafia and similar Italian secret societies. Indeed, the Sicilian Mafia refers to itself as the Honourable Society, because personal and family or tribal honour is the supreme value to be protected, and the vendetta is the means of settling disputes. Once again, the state – if it exists at all – is a common enemy, interfering in business that doesn't concern it.

And this is roughly how it was until relatively recent historical times in most of Europe, not to mention anywhere else. These days, people who end up in prison as a result of a criminal conviction are pretty unrepresentative of humanity in historical times. For example, the English system of common law – one of the oldest and most venerable in the modern world – began to develop its modern form, and slowly at that, only after the Norman Conquest in 1066. So what preceded it? Local customary law, enforced by local ad hoc tribunals, vendettas and so on. Even after the Normans came to Britain, and then to Ireland, the idea that an offence should be tested on the evidence and the guilty party, if guilt could be established by examining the circumstances of the offence, be deprived of his liberty by locking him up in a prison, would have – for a long time – have seemed pretty bizarre.

So how did these village tribunals determine guilt or innocence, assuming that they had any kind of process at all other than the vendetta? Well, there were things like trial by ordeal or trial by combat. Trial by ordeal meant inflicting on the suspect some sort of profound physical discomfort, a torture such as plunging his hand into boiling water or submitting him to the medieval equivalent of waterboarding – near drowning – and inferring guilt or innocence from how the poor devil survived the ordeal, if he did. Trial by combat was, on the other hand, a bully's charter, but it had the merit of allowing the strongest and most ruthless in a small, village society to rise to the top. Tribal societies such as those in Gaelic Ireland operated their chieftaincy laws in a similar manner, allowing the succession to be contested among cousins unto the third or fourth degree and may the best man win. He was more likely to be the meanest brute around than the deceased king's eldest son – who might well be an incompetent idiot – and thus he could keep the whole tribe safe.

Gradually, the beginnings of modern states begin to emerge, most notably in England and France. In Italy, the states were city-based rather than national enterprises, but the logic was the same. There was now a body of authority – very often endorsed and anointed by the papacy, the supreme arbiter of morality in Western Christianity – which gradually claimed coercive powers over the people under its protection. So the business of keeping the community safe passed from local strongmen and warlords to a remote, divinely sanctioned authority, and that royal authority made ever-growing aspects of human behaviour its business.

A state – whether a national state or a city state – claimed coercive powers and had the means to enforce them. It could raise troops to make war abroad or keep the peace at home; it could levy taxes and had the means to see that they were collected; it superintended a system of administration; and it created the criminal law.

Some criminal offences were obviously the business of the state, treason or rebellion for instance, for such things threatened to subvert the entire structure. Gradually, the idea took hold that certain things previously thought essentially private matters, such as murder or theft, were no such thing. They were offences against the moral order that the state existed to protect, and so they were taken out of the hands of private jurisdiction and relocated in the public square. Offences were no longer to be examined by primitive expedients such as trial by ordeal or combat, but by a process designed to establish the facts of the case, to be held in an open court according to a body of law. It was a process of reason rather than one of glorified superstition.

How were those found guilty under this new system to be punished? Under the old vendetta systems, blood money could be paid to a victim's family to avoid a feud – and this expedient was often resorted to. However, now that murder, for example, was a public crime rather than just a private matter between two families or tribes, there had to be some public punishment as decreed by law. So, there was physical mutilation – cutting off thieves' hands and other parts of the anatomy – exile, various exquisite tortures and, of course, the death penalty. This last was generally carried out in public, usually before an audience of enthusiastic onlookers, and was regarded by many as an unbeatable form of street theatre.

Then, gradually, it occurred to the authorities that deprivation of liberty was an appropriate punishment for certain crimes. Thus was formed the germ of the modern prison system. Instead of cruel traditional punishments, such as detaining a prisoner in a pillory or stocks, it was deemed appropriate simply to take offenders out of society, deprive them of their liberty and incarcerate them in a secure place until they were deemed to have paid their debt to society. The debt was now owed, not to the offended private party, whether family or tribe, but to society at large.

Medieval prisons were first built to house debtors and these places in time became known as marshalseas, after a notorious London debtors' prison. Over the centuries, the system developed further until by the 19th century it had assumed roughly the shape that we recognise today.

Kilmainham Gaol was one small part of that very large historical process, but it was destined to play an outsized part in the history of Ireland. An extraordinary number of patriotic Irish men and women, who gave their liberty – and sometimes their lives – in the cause of Irish freedom passed through its intimidating entrance. That is its claim on history and on our interest. There are prisons all over the place and few of them merit much more than a passing mention, footnotes in the development of the criminal law. But Kilmainham is, for Irish people, a site of sacred memory because of those who passed within its walls and those who died there.

The dead, of course, include most of the leaders of the Easter Rising of 1916. They were taken out, one by one, into the stonebreakers' yard in Kilmainham and placed before British firing squads. Winston Churchill once famously remarked: 'Grass grows over a battlefield, never over a scaffold.' And so it is here.

The old gaol has, in recent times, been superbly restored – it had, until the 1960s, been in a state of considerable decay – and is now in the care of the Office of Public Works (OPW), an Irish state body. The OPW has discharged its duty of care with exemplary sensitivity, with the result that Kilmainham Gaol is now one of the top tourist attractions in Dublin. This is all the more remarkable when you consider its location, in the inner suburbs to the west of the city – Dublin's less fashionable quarter. It is, by Dublin standards at least, relatively remote from the parts that attract most visitors – Trinity College and the Georgian squares and the fashionable area centred on Grafton Street and environs, all well to the east of Kilmainham.

Kilmainham has its claim on the imagination of all those visitors. Irish nationalism – the desire to be free of English rule – long antedated the days when the leaders of the 1916 Rising walked out to execution in the stonebreakers' yard. Those deaths, collectively, represented a transformative moment. An old order died and a new world, our world, was born.

Location

Now an inner suburb of Dublin, Kilmainham was originally a little settlement about three kilometres to the west of the small medieval town that grew up around Christ Church Cathedral. There were a number of such satellite villages at the outer reaches of the city of Dublin, which gradually – over time – expanded to embrace them and, indeed, bypass them, a process common to the development of most modern cities.

All of these outlying villages had some natural advantage, such as defensible high ground well above any flood line. So it was with Kilmainham. It stands about a kilometre south of the Liffey, which is still tidal at the nearest point. In a similar manner, other outlying settlements were likewise circumstanced: Drumcondra, to the north of the city, stood on rising ground, like Kilmainham; Ringsend, to the east, on the lower reaches of the Liffey, stood on a spit of land that remained high and dry above high water.

Opposite:
Christ Church
Cathedral.

The little settlement stood astride one of the principal early roads leading out of Dublin to the south-west, connecting with the flat lands of Kildare; beyond that it gave access to the interior and south of the island. This conjunction of circumstances, its secure hillside setting along an early trade route, together with its proximity to the small town – it's not possible to describe Dublin as a city until the 17th century – made it an obvious and attractive place of settlement.

So it proved, for we know that there was a monastery at Kilmainham as early as the seventh century. Invariably, any such institution in its turn attracted secular proto-villages adjacent to it. These were in no sense early towns, for there were no towns as such in Gaelic Ireland: that development awaited the arrival of the Danes after AD 795.

Still, the fact that there was anything at all there in an age before Dublin itself existed indicates that, even then, the area possessed some strategic value and significance. The monastery at Kilmainham did not survive the depredations of the Vikings and it vanished from history long before AD 1000.

It did, however, leave one shadowy figure. According to the Annals of the Four Masters – a compendium of early Irish history set down by Franciscan scholars in the 17th century – a learned monk in the Celtic monastery was known as the philosopher of Kilmainham. The Annals of the Four Masters recorded the date of his death as AD 782. We know nothing else about the philosopher of Kilmainham, but he is at least the first human that we can associate with this patch of rising ground above the flood plain of the Liffey.

The location provided one further natural advantage. Going the short distance downhill to what is now Islandbridge gave access to an ancient fording point across the river. This stood roughly at the tidal reach of the river and was later regarded as the western limit of the medieval town. Later again, it was developed into a weir, which can still be seen today.

The Annals of the Four Masters, by B. H. Holbrooke, 1846.

Derivation of the Name

The name of the district derives from the Irish name of the early Celtic monastery, Cill Mhaighneann. In Irish, the word Cill could indicate a church or a wood, more usually the former. It is the root of many Irish place names associated with monastic settlements, as in Kildare (Cill Dara, church of the oak). Quite who or what Mhaighneann was is uncertain, but it most likely was the name of either the founder or an early holy man of some distinction.

At any rate, the name stuck – and was anglicised to Kilmainham much later. The monastery disappeared. The sudden, brutal arrival of the Vikings in the late eighth century was one of the most consequential events in all of Irish history. They were raiders and traders, but critically they were town builders. They founded the early medieval town of Dublin, on the hill where Christ Church Cathedral stands today, drawing their long boats up on the sandy shore of the Liffey's south bank. They also pushed further upriver, towards the tidal reach at Islandbridge, where they were also able to beach their boats.

That gave the Vikings the access to Kilmainham that put an end to the monastery. Monasteries were an easy and tempting target for these raiders, being conspicuous centres of wealth and therefore obvious targets for plunder. There may even have been a small satellite Viking settlement in the vicinity of Islandbridge/Kilmainham in the ninth century, because a Viking burial ground has been discovered there by archaeologists. However, there is no certain evidence of any such settlement. There is no doubt about the burials, however, which are recognisably Viking in character. For example, the bodies were buried with grave goods, a practice forbidden by Christian usage. The burial ground echoes features found at other Viking sites in the general vicinity of Dublin.

Thanks to the Vikings, Kilmainham more or less disappears from history for a couple of centuries. The Vikings became part of the Irish mix, co-existing with the established Gaelic inhabitants and frequently fighting them. They didn't have things all their own way, however, for the Gaels proved to be their military equals as often as not. Thus it was that, by 1014 – one of the key dates in Irish history – the entire island of Ireland was a contested space, with various warlords, both Gaelic and Viking, constantly looking for advantage and more than able and willing to fight for it.

When the issue was joined in that fateful year, it was later misrepresented as a straight fight between Gaels and Vikings. It was not. There were Vikings engaged on both sides of the key battle, which was fought at Clontarf, to the east of the town. However, while the Battle of Clontarf was not the decisive event it was subseqently celebrated as, it was certainly a significant moment in Irish history. In the preparation for the battle, Kilmainham re-entered the historical frame.

It is time to meet one of the legendary figures in the Irish story: Brian Ború.

The bloody Battle of Clontarf in 1014 was a significant, if not decisive, engagement.

Brian Ború

Born around 940, Brian Ború at first was just a minor regional sub-king on the lower reaches of the Shannon, near the modern city of Limerick. By 980 he had fought his way to being king of Munster and was now a serious warlord. By the turn of the first millennium, he had imposed himself militarily on the rest of the island.

Brian Bórú was the twelfth son of his father, Cennétig. As a child he saw his mother, Bébinn, murdered by Viking raiders. In 1005, he declared that Armagh was the religious capital of all Ireland. The Book of Armagh named him 'Emperor of the Irish'.

There had been notional claims to a position of High King of Ireland, with various claimants. However, the high kingship was a fiction. No one in Gaelic Ireland ever managed to establish a central royal power, with a royal army, uniform enforcement of the law and an effective tax-gathering regime. There was no shame in this: it was the condition of most of Europe.

What made Brian Ború stand out was that he almost succeeded in achieving this, or at least in consolidating a process that might have made it possible. In reality, he was simply the most daring and successful warlord of them all. He was able to project his power over the whole island in the first decade of the new millennium, but it was as an overlord rather than as a proto-king. There was no sign of a state apparatus in Brian's Ireland.

The Battle of Clontarf in 1014 has been traditionally represented as the battle that kicked the Vikings out of Ireland. However, it was no such thing. Brian was by now in his 70s, a very long innings at the time. Moreover, he was an overlord, not a king, and those under his heel had grown increasingly resentful of his power.

According to legend, as Brodir, King of Man, fled from the battle he killed Brian Bórú. Brodir was caught and tortured to death.

What happened at Clontarf in 1014 was not a straightforward Irish versus Vikings head-to-head. It was a revolt of some Leinster sub-kings, with Viking support, against Brian. However, Brian also had some Viking support on his side, because the Vikings were no more tribally homogeneous than the Gaels.

Battle of Clontarf, oil on canvas painting by Hugh Frazer, 1826.

Clontarf was a pyrrhic victory for Brian. He lost his life; his son and grandson also died, and with them died the possibility – already remote – of a secure dynastic succession. It did not force out the Vikings, who remained kings of Dublin, on and off, for the next hundred years and more.

So, where does Kilmainham come into all this? It was a mustering point for some of Brian's troops coming up from the south and west: once again, its position along the principal road to and from the south made it a logical choice. It had other advantages: its uphill position made it relatively secure against surprise raids and its access to the river allowed the efficient dispatch of troops to the battle site away to the east.

It was simple geography. Not only was Dublin a little town on a hill, but all its satellites were similarly advantaged. Even Ringsend, away downriver – even farther east than Clontarf – was a little spit of dry land standing proud of the highest tides. Kilmainham was the most significant of these early satellites, being the closest to the walled town. It was a significant place.

St Patrick's Church, Ringsend. The village lay well to the east of the walled medieval town, but offered a safe anchorage for shipping.

The Order of St John

Far more than the Vikings, the arrival of the Normans in 1169 had an utterly transformative effect on Ireland. This event inserted the crown of England directly into Irish affairs for the first time, although it was as much by accident as design. The little town on the Liffey overtook Waterford to become the centre of royal power in Ireland, a position it was to hold for centuries.

Richard de Clare, better known as Strongbow, was king of Leinster and the most consequential Norman adventurer in Ireland. In 1175, he granted the lands at Kilmainham to the Knights Hospitallers of St John of Jerusalem – a papal order originally established for the medical assistance of Christians in the Holy Land, which later developed into a military establishment. They founded a hospital and several almshouses on the site.

Kilmainham's good location stood to it, for it occupied a ridge that commanded the view all the way east to the walled town, while remaining at once both distant and near. In a sense, the Order of St John – often erroneously confused with the Knights Templar, a separate and often rival papal military order – had an effect on the district not unlike that of the original Celtic monastery all those centuries earlier.

A suburb began to form. The area became noted for its mills. The Camac, a tributary of the Liffey, ran downhill nearby on its way to join the larger river and facilitated this development. However, as time passed, Kilmainham's relative distance had other effects. A county prison was established there, a nasty, insanitary dungeon in which unfortunates languished. It was the forerunner of the modern prison, the subject of this book.

The Marriage of Strongbow and Aoife, the monumental painting by Daniel Maclise in the National Gallery of Ireland.

Kilmainham was also the site of an ancient burial ground, now contained within the walls of the Royal Hospital, which became known as 'Bully's Acre'. Over the centuries, as parish churchyards took care of local burials, Bully's Acre became the least favoured graveyard in the city, receiving the remains of the poorest of the poor. Thus the name: in 18th-century Dublin slang, a bully was a thief or a thug. Bully's Acre did not close for burials until 1832.

Strongbow's choice of the bluff at Kilmainham for the land grant to the Knights Hospitallers of St John of Jerusalem was almost certainly governed by military considerations. By having a military order astride the

Portrait of Henry VIII, by Hans Holbein, 1537.

western approaches and defences of the capital, it commanded any possible rebel routes from the interior. It served a similar military purpose in later centuries.

The medieval world came to a sudden end in the 1530s, with England's break with the Church of Rome, the beginnings of the Reformation, and the development that bore most directly on the fortunes of Kilmainham: the dissolution of the monasteries. Just as the Vikings had put an end to the Celtic monastery, Henry VIII put an end to the Knights Hospitallers of St John of Jerusalem. The estates at Kilmainham were expropriated by the crown, thus ending almost 400 years of history.

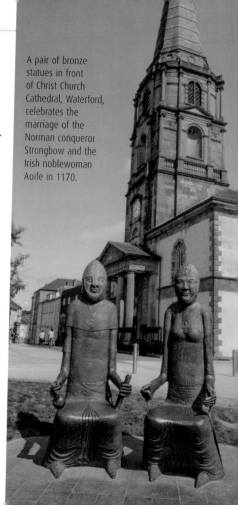

A pair of bronze statues in front of Christ Church Cathedral, Waterford, celebrates the marriage of the Norman conqueror Strongbow and the Irish noblewoman Aoife in 1170.

Dissolution and Summer Residence

Monasteries were rich foundations, often decadent and neglectful of the original spiritual purpose. As far back as Viking times, they had attracted the depredations and plunderings of those seaborne raiders. However, the Vikings were pagans, from whom nothing better could be expected. It was quite another thing for a Christian king to close them down, physically destroy them and expropriate their assets and riches, transferring legal title of these confiscated properties to loyalists and other favoured courtiers and supporters.

Yet that is what Henry VIII and his strongman, Thomas Cromwell, did in the 1530s and early 1540s. There had been tensions between popes and kings throughout Europe for centuries – with each side vying for ultimate supremacy – but nothing on this scale had ever been attempted before. Later on, a similar process marked the French and Russian

Thomas Cromwell, by Hans Holbein, 1532–33 (detail).

Revolutions, but this Tudor upheaval was the first and was on such a scale as to possess the shock value that attaches to all sudden and unprecedented events.

The monastery of the Knights Hospitallers of St John of Jerusalem was suppressed in 1542. There was an attempted revival under the brief reign of the Catholic Queen Mary Tudor (1553–58), but she was succeeded by her half-sister, the Protestant Elizabeth, who reigned for 45 years. That settled the matter, and the lands at Kilmainham were vested in the crown.

Prior to the Tudor revolution, Ireland had effectively been governed in the king's name by Hiberno-English aristocrats. These were effectively local warlords, usually of the House of Kildare; they were descendants of the original Norman invaders of the late 12th century. Ireland was awkwardly distant from England – and especially from the seat of power in the south-east around London – so it made sense, including financial sense, to devolve Irish administration to trusted strongmen.

Queen Elizabeth I, The Armada Portrait, Woburn Abbey, England, by an unknown artist, c.1588 (detail).

Irish mercenaries in
Europe, drawing by
Albrecht Dürer, 1521.

That arrangement had broken down irretrievably with the doomed rebellion of Silken Thomas – the last of the great magnate earls of Kildare – in 1534. Thereafter, the English crown had to take a more direct hand in the governance of Irish affairs. A succession of chief governors and senior officials came to Ireland to administer the country – or as much of it as lay within the king's writ, which was not nearly as much as they would have wished – by what we would now call direct rule.

What had been the priory house was turned into a suite of summer residences for the chief governor and his senior officials. It is worth remembering just how extensive the entire place was. It included not just the modern buildings of Kilmainham Gaol and courthouse but all the land later enclosed by the walls of the Royal Hospital, so the English officials had plenty of room for their summer holiday accommodation.

As before, the presence of a settlement, even on a seasonal basis, encouraged micro-suburbs to form in its shadow. This happened in Kilmainham, as it had in the past, but we also get a first glimpse at this time of what were later to develop into the suburbs of Inchicore, a little further west, and – down the hill towards the river – Islandbridge.

Kilmainham had made the greatest leap in its history, from a religious to a secular site. It is that new status that dominates the rest of our story.

The capture of the FitzGeralds, uncles of Thomas FitzGerald, also known as Silken Thomas, during the The Kildare rebellion of 1534–35.

The Royal Hospital

The first great survey of classical Dublin was published in 1952 by the architectural historian Maurice Craig. It was simply titled *Dublin 1660–1860*. The standard modern history of the entire city is David Dickson's *Dublin: The Making of a Capital City* (2014). Dickson's book runs to 563 pages of main text, yet has already reached 1662 – also Craig's effective starting date – by page 79. That year is important for both writers for the same reason: it marked the arrival of James Butler, 1st Duke of Ormond, as viceroy. In effect, Ormond started the modern city.

Dublin became the permanent seat of parliament, which had previously been peripatetic. Suburban development north across the Liffey and west towards Kilmainham extended the city's footprint. Where there was only one bridge over the river in 1660, there were five by 1683. We have Ormond to thank for the Phoenix Park, Grafton St and St Stephen's Green. There was a sustained building boom, not least in churches. The greatest of all these developments was in Kilmainham.

The 1680s saw the construction of the Royal Hospital, the first great post-Renaissance classical building in the city. It was built towards the eastern end of the old priory lands and was later physically separated from the modern gaol and courthouse at the start of Inchicore Road by the construction in the late 18th century of the South Circular Road, which made a right angle with Inchicore Road.

This noble building was designed for the accommodation of old soldiers who had fallen on hard times, either through injury or illness. It was modelled on Les Invalides in Paris and the Chelsea

Sir William Robinson, by Godfrey Kneller, 1693.

The Royal Hospital, Kilmainham.

Hospital in London. It was designed by the surveyor-general of Ireland, Sir William Robinson, who also designed Marsh's Library beside St Patrick's Cathedral and did important restoration work in Dublin Castle following a fire in 1684.

Nothing like it had been seen in Dublin before. The Royal Hospital stands around an internal quadrangle, perfectly harmonious and classically regular. A tower comprising a somewhat attenuated spire gives the building vertical definition. It could accommodate 300 old soldiers in comfort. It also had a feature that is rare in Dublin: the Huguenot wood carver, James Tabary, produced a spectacular exhibition of his craft in the baroque carvings he provided for the chapel. Dublin is a city almost devoid of baroque features: Tabary's work in the hospital chapel is one of the few such examples that the city possesses.

There is an irony here. The whole history of Dublin since 1660 has been a steady push eastwards from the medieval core around Christ Church towards Dublin Bay. Thus the movement of fashion, first into the north-east quadrant around O'Connell Street and Mountjoy Square, and later across the river to the south-east around St Stephen's Green and Merrion Square. There it has stayed, followed later by outer suburban development wrapping around the bay. As one report of 1780 noted: 'the western side ... remote from the sea ...

is chiefly inhabited by merchants and mechanicks.'
Nevertheless the first great secular, classical building
– announcing the start of the city's heroic age – was
built to the west.

The chapel, Royal
Hospital, Kilmainham.

Gallows Hill and the Old Gaol

The site occupied by Kilmainham Gaol today was once known as Gallows Hill. The name is a giveaway: it was a place of public execution, a practice that continued for a while after the modern gaol was built. Public executions slowed from about the 1820s, as they moved inside the gaol itself, although the last public hanging was as late as 1865.

The construction of the South Circular Road and the enclosing of the lands of the Royal Hospital at Kilmainham now physically separated Gallows Hill from the rest of the old priory lands. The site of the future prison stood at the head of the road leading to the Black Lion Turnpike, now known as Inchicore Road. (The old name is commemorated in the name of a well-known public house in Inchicore, the Black Lion.)

Not enough is known about the old county gaol that stood nearby. By such accounts as we have, it was simply a four-room dungeon that served as a dumping ground for miscreants of all kinds. There was no thought of rehabilitation or any other modern consideration, such as was gradually to inform penal practice as the 19th century wore on.

The old gaol appears to have been situated by the banks of the River Camac, roughly at the junction of the modern Old Kilmainham

Irish gentlemen descend into an underground brothel near Dirty Lane, Dublin, with beds and cheap victuals. Engraving, published 1829.

and Brookfield Road. We know that in the 1780s it was visited by John Howard, the great prison reformer. More than anyone, he was instrumental in effecting the reform of traditional places of incarceration and their replacement by modern penitentiaries. His influence was doubtless instrumental in seeing the closure of the old county gaol and the movement towards the building of the new county prison on Gallows Hill.

As in every other contemporary city, the 18th-century population increase brought in its wake a huge rise in crime. Thefts and burglaries were rife, brothels flourished – and were predictable occasions for violence and worse. No fewer than 242 people were hanged in Dublin

Irish gentlemen descend into an underground brothel near Dirty Lane, Dublin, with beds and cheap victuals. Engraving, published 1829.

between 1780 and 1795, most of them for theft. Most prosecutions were taken privately and were expensive; there was no state prosecution structure. Parish watches were corrupt and unreliable, while the greatest migratory pressure fell on the poorest parishes with the fewest resources and, therefore, the feeblest watch systems. Everyone had a price. At one point, even the city executioner was convicted of armed robbery.

A Sketch from Nature, William Paulet Carey, January 24, 1784.

Prisons were dumping grounds for thieves, swindlers, bullies, brothel-keepers and prostitutes – in short, all the riff-raff who represented the criminal underbelly of Dublin in its most glittering, golden age. Although precise statistics are unknown, there is little doubt that, in the 18th century, Ireland was more violent than England; one estimate gives an Irish murder rate four times that of the larger island. Jailers were notoriously venal, very often requiring a fee on entry, further payments for favours (including those of women) and a further fee on release, even though all other requirements of the law had been satisfied: the departing prisoner was thus held hostage.

However, attitudes to crime and punishment were changing slowly. It was a process that went on through the early 19th century, especially between 1780 and 1840, when the prison reform movement showed extraordinary zeal. By the late 18th century, there was a sense that simply dumping offenders in filthy, insanitary, noisome holes-in-the-ground was no longer good enough. A reform movement developed. No one was more important in driving this forward than prison reformer John Howard.

A Sketch from Nature,
William Paulet Carey,
January 24, 1784.

John Howard

John Howard (1726–1790) was the son of a well-to-do London merchant. He spent some time in French prisons in the 1750s, having been captured en route to Portugal. This experience prompted his lifelong interest in prisons and prison reform. In due time, he returned to England and became High Sheriff of Bedfordshire. Like many a man with an evangelical zeal for reform, he was regarded by many contemporaries as eccentric, if not actually unstable.

John Howard by Mather Brown, 1789.

Posterity has been much kinder to him, and so were many of his contemporaries – for he was horrified by the state of prisons in Bedfordshire. From there, he began a nationwide tour of prisons, publishing a seminal book on the subject in 1777 and framing two reforming acts of parliament, which mark the origin point of modern penology.

Howard's work was anticipated by that of the great Italian prison reformer Cesare di Beccaria, whose *Essay on Crimes and Punishments* had been published in 1764. It was widely translated and an English edition appeared in Dublin as early as 1767. John Howard was influenced by Beccaria, whose proposed reforms – already familiar in Ireland because of the translation of his book – he endorsed. Howard visited Ireland six times between 1775 and his death. His celebrity in the country was such that he was awarded an honorary LL.D by Trinity College (to add to the Freedom of the City of London).

He also visited many Irish jails and bridewells, finding them even more primitive and horrifying than anything he had found in England (and those were appalling). Indeed, he compared

John Howard (1726–1790), anonymous artist, 1883.

Irish conditions to those in the interior of Russia – an especially unflattering comparison. He had indeed travelled as far as Russia, and it was there that he died at the age of 63.

In the meantime, we can be certain that Howard had visited the old prison at Kilmainham. He condemned it for all the conventional reasons and urged the building of a new kind of prison. This was the intellectual fountainhead of the new prison that was constructed on Gallows Hill after Howard's death. It may look grim to us, given all its sinister historical associations, but it still represented a hugely humane step forward from the stygian hellhole down the road. Its elevated location alone allowed for the circulation of a greater amount of fresh air, a key consideration for Howard, and one that would have been of enormous benefit to the prisoners incarcerated within its walls.

Take just one thing that we take wholly for granted in prisons: single cells for each prisoner. That was one of Howard's headline proposals, regarded by many at the time as impossibly idealistic and – as with so many of these things – completely normal to the generations that followed.

Without Howard, it is almost certain that the complex we see now on what had been Gallows Hill, with all its history and fable, would not exist – or at least not in its actual present form. Everything starts with the idea, and the idea was Howard's. His name echoes to this day in the Howard League for Penal Reform, the leading such group in the UK. After the idea came building blocks and mortar – Kilmainham Gaol was built in the 1790s.

Statue of philanthropist and prison reformer John Howard (1726–1790), by Sir Alfred Gilbert (1854–1934). Located in Bedford, England.

Kilmainham Gaol Opens

The west wing of what is now Kilmainham Gaol opened in 1796, almost ten years after its construction. The more modern east wing did not follow until the 1860s, although a symmetrical wing had been built on this site originally. While the west wing seems forbidding in contrast to the east, it still represented a considerable advance on the old gaol that it had replaced. The corridors in the west wing are narrow and gloomy, but the critical ambition of one cell per prisoner was achieved there from the start. That alone marked a huge step forward, even when not always achieved.

That said, it was still a place that no one would choose to be in. The prison may have been new but the administration and regime were very much in the old style. The jailers, or turnkeys, as they were known, were corrupt and biddable. The poorest prisoners were guaranteed the worst quarters and could not even hope to solicit alms from outsiders in order to bribe the turnkeys into upgrading them to better accommodation as they had been able to do in the old jail.

As a general rule, women were treated worse than men, especially in the matter of bedding. Where men might be fortunate enough to get cots to sleep on, women usually were left to sleep on straw. Inevitably, the straw was alive with ticks and vermin. Overall, the early prison was an improvement on what had preceded it, but while it was one thing to will architectural change, it was quite another to effect the cultural change in prison management that should have accompanied it. It was still a house of detention and punishment; there was no thought of rehabilitation.

Kilmainham Gaol, now run by the Office of Public Works (OPW).

A corridor in Kilmainham Gaol.

Most of the criminals held in Kilmainham were petty offenders sentenced by judges and magistrates in court. Thus, petty thieves, drunks, and those convicted of assault and prostitution were the prison's stock-in trade in the early days. Debtors also found themselves there, although they usually succeeded in being released if they were able, by one means or another – usually through the generosity of a well-disposed third party – to discharge the debt.

In some cases, the exit fees, which continued to be demanded by the more unscrupulous turnkeys, were an additional imposition. Corrupt practices such as this were supposed to be a thing of the past with the move from the old to the new jail, but inevitably it took time for a new culture of prison management to bed in. Practices that had been commonplace for generations were hardly going to disappear on demand, although the gradual movement towards a more modern and humane system of prison management could not have happened without the physical infrastructure of the new prison being there to sustain it.

Kilmainham generally did not house more serious prisoners, except while on remand awaiting trial. Murder and other felonies usually resulted in execution or transportation to the remote colonies. It comes as a surprise, therefore, to discover that the first 'celebrity' prisoner was not at all a part of the city's low life but was an honoured and wealthy citizen of another city. In 1796, the year the new prison opened on Gallows Hill, Henry Joy McCracken found himself incarcerated within.

A view of a British colony from a journal kept on board the *Minerva* transport, from Ireland to New South Wales and Bengal, by John Washington Price, Surgeon, May, 1798-June, 1800. Note the hanged man on the small island.

Henry Joy McCracken

Henry Joy McCracken was the first in a long line of distinguished nationalist patriots to do time in Kilmainham. He came from that subset of Irish revolutionaries most directly affected by the parliamentary reform movement and especially by the French Revolution.

Henry Joy McCracken (1767–1798), by Sarah Cecilia Harrison (1863–1941).

The Joys and the McCrackens were part of Belfast's bourgeois Presbyterian business elite. The commerce of the town was dominated by Presbyterians – the Anglicans preferred land to commerce, which they considered *déclassé* – and in all this they left their mark. Francis Joy (1697–1790) was the founder-proprietor of the *Belfast News-Letter* in 1737. It remains the longest continuously published newspaper in the British Isles.

His two sons, Henry and Robert Joy, succeeded him in due time as proprietors and editors. One of their sisters, Anne, married another member of this Presbyterian mercantile caste, Captain John McCracken. He was a shipowner and had a number of ancillary businesses associated with shipping. He imported the first bales of cotton to the town and built its first cotton mill, an early harbinger of the Industrial Revolution. His marriage produced seven children, among them Henry Joy McCracken and his sister Mary Ann.

Henry Joy McCracken was born in 1767. By the age of 22 he had been placed in charge of his father's cotton mill. However, that year – 1789 – was the headiest year of the century. The French Revolution had an immediate and urgent appeal to Ulster Presbyterians like McCracken: his was a highly literate, self-composed, well-educated community, chafing under the condescension of Anglican grandees. It was exactly the kind of aspirant, bourgeois community that felt put upon by the rigidities of the *ancien régime*.

It is hardly a surprise that a lively young man of his time and place should be drawn to revolutionary endeavours. This was the glad dawn of the French Revolution: the horrors of the Terror were still well in the future. Gradually, together with other like-minded young men

Liberty Leading the People, by Eugène Delacroix (1798–1863), 1830.

of that generation, he was drawn to radical politics and eventually became a member of the Society of United Irishmen, of which the best-known figure was Theobald Wolfe Tone.

Everything changed when Britain went to war with France in 1793; it was to be almost continuously at war for the next 22 years. Suddenly, radical flirtation with French Revolutionary principles could be denominated as sedition. It was precisely for this offence that Henry Joy was captured and incarcerated in Kilmainham in 1796. He spent more than a year there.

When he was released, he became commander of the doomed provincial rebellion in Ulster in 1798. He failed in an attempt to flee to America, refused to inform on colleagues and was hanged in Belfast after a perfunctory trial. His sister, Mary Ann, accompanied him to the gallows. She lived long, into her 90s, a champion of liberal causes and a major source for R. R. Madden's history of the 1798 Rebellion, the first major history of that tumultuous event.

Mary Ann McCracken, sister of Henry Joy McCracken.

Henry Joy
McCracken was
hanged at Belfast
market-house on
17 June 1798.

The 1798 Rebellion

The rebellion in Ulster in 1798 was confined to the two eastern counties of Antrim and Down. It was a minor, localised affair compared to the events in Leinster. The rebellion was planned on a national scale – the Ulster outbreak factored in as a part of it – but it was betrayed by police spies and informers. Most of the national leadership of the United Irishmen were arrested in March. When, eventually, a rebellion began in late May, it was largely confined to the counties of the south-east, especially Wexford.

It lasted for about a month. Early rebel successes were insufficient to break the rebellion out of County Wexford, and government troops eventually defeated the rebels in a decisive battle at Vinegar Hill, just above the town of Enniscorthy.

The result was, inevitably, a huge number of prisoners and a consequent pressure on the prison system. The numbers incarcerated in Kilmainham were far greater than the prison was designed to

Defeat at Vinegar Hill, illustrated by George Cruikshank (1845).

hold. Their names are recorded in great detail in the prison registers.

One prisoner, Father John Martin, was an Augustinian friar from Drogheda. In 1797, he had taken the United Irish oath – although he claimed that it was no oath, which would have been treasonous in law and, even worse, offensive to Rome; rather, he claimed merely to have affirmed. At any rate, he was an important minor figure in the councils of the United Irishmen. His skills as a preacher were deployed in the cause.

The national character of the planned rebellion was compromised by the early

Wolfe Tone is captured.

culling of the leadership in March. Early defeats on the margins of
Leinster kept Dublin safe and effectively confined the rebels to Wexford
and, for a while, the southern tip of County Wicklow. Father Martin
maintained contact with some of the local leaders until his luck ran out
and he was captured by the yeomanry. He was lodged in Kilmainham.

He was interrogated in very rough fashion by the Dublin city
militia and was quickly broken. He denounced the United Irishmen
and denied any intention of taking up arms himself. He may well have
incriminated others. At any rate, the authorities found him useful and
maintained him in the prison. He was still there in 1800, when he made
an unsuccessful plea to be released. He eventually escaped in 1801,
climbing down a ladder (did he have help?) and going on the run.
Despite a price on his head, he was not recaptured.

No subsequent record of Father Martin exists in any Irish source,
including the records of his own Augustinian order. It is most likely
that he made his way to a Catholic country in Europe, there to
disappear from history. He was only one of the hundreds of wretched
prisoners incarcerated in Kilmainham in the aftermath of the 1798
Rebellion, held in horrible conditions for which the prison on Gallows
Hill had never been designed.

There was to be an aftershock.

Thomas Addis Emmet

Many men who had been involved with the United Irish cause, albeit sometimes on the margins, were to see the inside of Kilmainham. As might be expected after an insurrection as potent as that of 1798, the authorities panicked and were not too fussy about whom they picked up. There was a wholesale round-up of anyone suspected of United Irish sympathies. The names of most of these detainees are known, thanks to the well-kept prison registers, and there are some that still resonate even after all this time.

Thomas Addis Emmet (1764–1827), by Samuel Morse (1791–1872) (detail).

Thomas Addis Emmet (1764-1827) was the elder brother of the more fabled Robert. A scion of a solidly bourgeois family, he took his primary degree from Trinity in 1783 and then studied medicine in Edinburgh, where he graduated the following year. He practised in London and on the continent for a while, but his life was changed by the death of his eldest brother, Christopher Temple Emmet, a rising star at the Irish Bar and generally regarded as the brightest of a bright brood.

Persuaded by his father, Thomas now switched careers; he took a law degree in Trinity and attended Lincoln's Inn in London. His practice at the Bar flourished. An Anglican, he married into a Presbyterian family.

All through these formative years, the pulse of European politics had been racing. The decisive moment came in France in 1789, after which the world was never the same again. As with many educated middle-class people, Thomas Emmet was caught up in the intellectual ferment. In 1792, he joined the Society of the United Irishmen and was influential in its counsels. He was regarded as one of the more prominent members of the society; as government crackdowns hardened following the declaration of war between Britain and France in 1793, Thomas denounced these measures and defended some of the radicals who had been charged in the courts.

Thomas was on the moderate wing of the United Irishmen, pinning his hopes for change on a substantial French invasion. Such an invasion force

Robert Emmet.

made it to Bantry Bay in December 1796 but could not effect a landing because of unseasonal contrary winds. It was one of the great might-have-beens: 15,000 of the finest troops in Europe could have strolled into Cork, but they never made it to shore in the first place.

As government repression increased, so did the more radical voices in the United Irish movement, calling for a popular uprising. This eventually happened in May and June of 1798, but in the meantime, Thomas Addis Emmet had been rounded up as part of a government trawl of radicals, which is how he came to be lodged in Kilmainham. While there, he wrote a history of English rule in Ireland which was published many years later. After his release, he was sent to Scotland, from where he made his way to Brussels.

Thomas Addis Emmet finally emigrated to the United States in 1804, where he resumed his law practice with considerable success for the rest of his career.

The End of the Irish Invasion, or The Destruction of the French Armada, satirical print by James Gillray, 1797.

The Brothers Sheares

If Thomas Addis Emmet survived the rebellion of 1798, the brothers John and Henry Sheares, barristers from Cork, were not so lucky. They both paid with their lives. Like so many men who were influential in the United Irishmen, John and Henry Sheares were in no sense from the bottom of the heap; on the contrary, by the standards of Ireland of the time they were children of privilege.

Henry Sheares.

The Sheares family was well connected. The brothers' father, a banker, had been an MP, and Henry, the elder of the two brothers, was an army officer – thus fulfilling a dream never realised by Wolfe Tone, who had hankered after the military life – before being called to the Bar. His younger brother John followed him to Trinity and the Bar. Theirs was a small, interconnected world.

In 1792, the brothers went to Paris where they made the acquaintance of leading revolutionaries and were present at the execution of Louis XVI in

January 1793. On returning to Dublin, they shared lodgings and lived comfortably. They had inherited some money and they each generated a good living at the Bar. As with so many of their kind, they were attracted to the United Irishmen, and they joined the society in 1793.

Henry, the more moderate of the pair, became president of the society, while John was a member of a committee drafting a proposal for parliamentary reform. They formed a branch of the United Irishmen in their native Cork, where Henry also stood as an election candidate in 1795.

John Sheares.

By then, the United Irishmen had been suppressed and driven underground and was thick with informers and government spies. The authorities were, therefore, well aware of the Sheares brothers and their activities. Like Thomas Addis Emmet, they defended well-known radicals in the courts. Indeed, despite the professional risks that they ran, they hardly bothered to conceal their political allegiances. Both remained active in the movement, especially after the capture of Lord

Edward FitzGerald and other members of the Leinster directory in March 1798.

Both brothers were arrested in May 1798 and charged with high treason, the principal evidence against them being a revolutionary document written in John's hand that was found in his house. Although this did not directly incriminate Henry, both were convicted despite the best efforts of a distinguished legal team.

The sentence, of course, was death. Their last days were spent in confinement in Kilmainham Gaol, adding to the ever-growing list of Irish patriots incarcerated therein. It was from Kilmainham that they

were led to execution. They were hanged publicly outside Newgate Prison, their corpses were beheaded and their remains were deposited in a vault in nearby St Michan's Church. They were the first United Irishmen to pay the supreme penalty.

The arrest of Edward FitzGerald, by George Cruickshank, 1845.

The crypt at St Michan's Church in Dublin is famous
for its mummified medieval residents.

Michael Dwyer

Michael Dwyer was another distinguished republican from 1798 who found himself lodged in Kilmainham Gaol. He was from County Wicklow, the mountainous county immediately south of Dublin which had been a thorn in the flesh of the English governments in the city on and off for centuries. In the later 1790s, the Society of United Irishmen took root in County Wicklow and at some point Michael Dwyer became a member.

When the rebellion broke out in late May 1798, Dwyer, together with other local United men, went south towards County Wexford, the main seat of the rebellion. He fought at the second Battle of Arklow, just inside the Wicklow border, on 9 June. The decisive action of this engagement was a charge by the rebels across open ground in an attempt to reach the entrenched lines of the defending soldiers. However, they had too much ground to cover against well-prepared government fire. Rebel losses were huge and the

Arklow in the 1840s.

entire attack failed to reach its objective. It faltered and then broke up altogether. Further similar efforts ended the same way.

It was a disastrous loss for the rebels, following as it did hard on the heels of the defeat a few days earlier at New Ross in the south-west of County Wexford. They had failed to break out of Wexford twice, once to the north at Arklow and again to the west at New Ross. The rebellion was now confined to Wexford, and Wexford alone.

The rebel forces were crushed by the end of June, and Dwyer took refuge in his native heath in the Wicklow Mountains, tending to wounded United men and participating in a guerrilla campaign under the leadership of a remarkable commander, Joseph Holt, which continued for the rest of the year. Holt also spent time in Kilmainham. When Holt accepted government terms, Dwyer became the leading captain in his place. He fought in a series of defensive battles and skirmishes against encroaching government forces.

In 1802, Dwyer joined the conspiracy that led to Robert Emmet's rising but, in a muddle all too typical of that ill-fated

Michael Dwyer.

adventure, a breakdown in communication meant that Dwyer and his band did not make it to Dublin to join the rebellion. By now Dwyer, a married man with a growing family, was well known to the authorities and they applied pressure, not just on him but on his extended family.

A deal was struck, at which point Dwyer was lodged in Kilmainham while the details were finalised. He was transported to New South Wales along with members of his family and other United sympathisers. He arrived in Sydney late in 1806 and received a grant of land. He had mixed fortunes in Australia, first being arrested on charges of sedition, then released. Within a few years he had been appointed chief constable of a town near Sydney and received an even larger grant of land. However, further charges ruined him financially and he died in 1825 after a spell in a debtors' prison.

Illustration by George Cruikshank. At the Battle of Arklow, Father Michael Murphy, a general with the United Irishmen, convinced his followers that the British Army bullets were harmless and that he could catch them. This inspired his men to attack, but Father Murphy was killed.

Robert Emmet

Robert Emmet (1778–1803) was the last of the establishment radicals of the 1790s, of whom Theobald Wolfe Tone was the most celebrated. Emmet was the son of a well-known Dublin physician and acquired a reputation as an orator while a student at Trinity College. However, he was expelled from Trinity when the authorities cracked down on suspected radicals in the fraught lead-up to the rebellion of 1798.

Robert Emmet.

Opposite: 1st Viscount Kilwarden, Lord Chief-Justice of Ireland murdered in his coach on 23 July 1803 by Irish Nationalists during the abortive Dublin rising inspired by Robert Emmett.

When the rebellion failed, the radicals re-grouped. Emmet, young and charismatic, quickly rose towards the top of these conspiratorial circles. The group, which included senior survivors of 1798, began to stockpile arms in preparation for another attempt. Likewise, they recruited fighting men.

A rising was planned for the late summer of 1803. The intention was to capture Dublin Castle and other significant buildings in Dublin, in the hope that this would trigger a nationwide rebellion. Alas, everything went wrong. Although the original

plan seems hopelessly naive in retrospect, it was compromised by every kind of bad luck and disorganisation. A premature explosion at an arms dump alerted the authorities to the fact that something was afoot and caused Emmet to bring forward the date of the rising.

What followed was less a rising than an affray. Only a few hundred men mustered in Thomas Street. Many of them were drunk, poorly armed and in no sense under proper military orders. They attacked the carriage of the unfortunate Lord Kilwarden, a notably liberal judge – at least by the contemporary standards of the Irish bench – and murdered him.

After a couple of hours of street affray, the whole thing fell apart. The 'rising' was quickly suppressed by troops. Emmet fled. He hid in the Wicklow Mountains, where he was discovered after about a month and brought to trial in Dublin on 19 September 1803. The conviction for high treason was a foregone conclusion. Out of this debacle, Emmet rescued himself for immortality. He wished to protect Sarah Curran, the young woman he loved, and offered his silence in the dock to the authorities in return for a promise not to pursue or prosecute her. They refused, so Emmet spoke.

Emmet replying to the verdict of high treason, September 19, 1803

It was, by any standard, a spellbinding piece of oratory, throwing down a challenge to later generations of revolutionaries that enchanted many, not least Pádraig Pearse. It was known all over the world; Abraham Lincoln knew it by heart. Emmet, knowing that his life was forfeit, did not put a tooth in it: 'Our object was to effect a break with England.' After a trial that had lasted all day, he was duly convicted and removed to Kilmainham, there to spend the last night of his life. He wrote some final letters, one in particular to the great lawyer John Philpot Curran, father of Sarah, in which his anguish over her was his prevailing emotion.

At 1 pm the following day, he was led from the condemned cell in Kilmainham to the place of execution in Thomas Street, where he was hanged and beheaded. His speech from the dock had secured his place in the Irish republican pantheon, where it remains secure, but more than that, his memory was loved in the Irish nationalist tradition. The word is not too strong.

In the most famous Kilmainham execution to take place outside the prison, Robert Emmet was hanged in Thomas Street, Dublin. The crowd was estimated at 40,000.

Anne Devlin

Anne Devlin (1780–1851) was an Irish republican, housekeeper to Robert Emmet and cousin of two leading United Irish rebels: Michael Dwyer and Arthur Devlin.

Anne Devlin (1780–1851) came from a County Wicklow family with United Irish connections, for which known associations the yeomanry destroyed their family home at the height of the 1798 rebellion. Her immediate family was not 'out' in 1798 – although cousins were – but they gave shelter to rebels on the run after the defeat at Arklow. The natural line of retreat for the defeated was into the fastnesses of the Wicklow Mountains. It was in these mountains that Anne Devlin acted as a courier for the rebels, who included her cousin Michael Dwyer.

Her father was imprisoned without charge for three years following the destruction of his house. When he was released, the whole family moved north, to

Rathfarnham on the southern outskirts of Dublin. Anne went to work as a housekeeper in the home of their new neighbour, Robert Emmet. She was committed to the same revolutionary cause as Emmet, knew of the plans for his doomed rising and carried messages for him.

The rising failed and Emmet came back, first to Rathfarnham, then into the Wicklow Mountains. He was eventually arrested when he returned to the city. In the meantime, the yeomanry had once again raided the Devlin house. They had every reason to believe that Anne knew of Emmet's whereabouts – as indeed she did, for she also acted as courier for him during this time – and used rough methods of interrogation to get her to talk. She kept silent.

A cell at Kilmainham.

For this, she and 21 members of her immediate family were taken into custody and incarcerated in Kilmainham Gaol. One of her brothers died there. Despite solitary confinement and the various sweeteners offered to her, she refused to divulge any information about Emmet. She remained faithful to Emmet's memory long after his execution, when she might have had every excuse to talk. Instead, she endured three years in prison, mainly at Kilmainham, but latterly at Dublin Castle. Naturally, her health suffered.

For all that, she managed to reconstruct her life after her release, probably with financial assistance from Emmet's friends, who admired her honour and constancy. She married and had children. She appears to have made a living as a laundress, again working some of the time for families that remembered Robert Emmet with affection. Late in life, she found herself living in straitened circumstances in John's Lane, just off Thomas Street, the site of Emmet's rebellion.

In old age, she gave evidence to R. R. Madden, the first historian of the United Ireland movement, thus providing an invaluable historical link, considering that so many of the principals in the United movement were by then long since dead. When she herself died, it was Madden who arranged for her remains to be buried in a prominent position in Glasnevin Cemetery.

She entered the pantheon of Irish patriot heroes by virtue of her honourable silences. In the face of torture and inducements, and despite being a person of slender means covering for one who was far higher on the social scale, she remained steadfast in her loyalty to Emmet. She was the Flora MacDonald of Ireland: as MacDonald protected Bonnie Prince Charlie after the disaster of Culloden, so did Anne Devlin protect Emmet.

Memorial plaque for Anne Devlin on the bridge at Aughrim in County Wicklow.

Thomas Russell

Thomas Russell is one of the more intriguing figures of the revolutionary period. Remembered, especially in Ulster where he spent much of his time, as 'The Man from God Knows Where', he spent more time in prison than any of them.

Russell (1767–1803) was born in County Cork, the son of an army officer. All his life he was religious and toyed with a clerical career before joining the army in India. He distinguished himself there and when he returned to Dublin in 1787 he was able to live a life of ease in the Royal Hospital, Kilmainham.

Then he met Wolfe Tone. They shared not just an affinity for radical politics – in the spirit of the times – but they genuinely liked each other. He resumed his army career and was posted to Belfast where, despite his army status but probably because of the social cachet it brought him, he was soon well known in local society. Given the nature of Belfast in the 1790s, that meant he rubbed shoulders with radicals inspired by the events in France. Among his friends were Henry Joy McCracken and his sister Mary Ann.

He was a founder member of the United

Irishmen and the only one to see its cause all the way from foundation to the collapse of Emmet's rebellion in 1803. Despite his increasing immersion in radical politics, he was for a while a magistrate in County Tyrone. He and Wolfe Tone remained close and collaborated on forward plans; in 1793 Russell became secretary of the Dublin United movement.

That was the year that everything changed, as Britain found itself at war with revolutionary France. Despite his role in Dublin, Russell spent more and more time in Belfast, writing pamphlets and newspaper articles. In 1794, he became librarian at the Belfast Society for Promoting Knowledge, the forerunner of the Linen Hall Library, one of that city's great cultural ornaments. His politics, like those of many others, were radicalised by events. He travelled widely to spread the United message and made contact with the Defenders, a lower-class agrarian secret society.

Eventually, Russell was appointed commander of the United troops in County Down, which naturally brought him at last to the attention of the authorities. In 1796, he was arrested and charged with high treason. That is when he saw the inside of Kilmainham Gaol, although most of his prison time was spent in Dublin's Newgate prison. He was held for six years without trial, which is all the more surprising considering the nature of the charge that he was facing.

Instead, the government responded to his declining health by sending him to a less rigorous prison in Scotland, where he regained his strength. He was released in 1802 and went to Paris. He continued to press the revolutionary cause, and in 1803 Robert Emmet summoned him back to Dublin to assist in the planned rebellion. Emmet asked Russell to take charge in Ulster, but the atmosphere there had been greatly changed by the events of 1798 and there was no mobilisation. Russell travelled back to Dublin to help the beleaguered Emmet, was captured and hanged at Downpatrick. He was the last of the United Irishmen to perish on the scaffold.

The arrest of Thomas Russell in 1796.

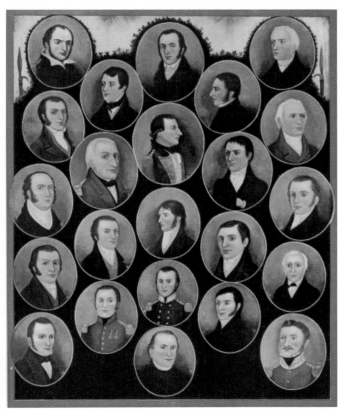

Leaders of the United Irishmen, 1798 and 1803.

County Prison

The distinction between a county prison and a city prison was an administrative one, depending on the nature of the superintending authority. Under the law, each county in Ireland had to have a jail, situated in the county town and overseen by the local grand jury. If the town was big enough – as in Dublin's case – there would also be a city jail. In Dublin, that was Newgate. Moreover, there were also marshalseas or debtors' prisons, and bridewells, where petty offenders were held on remand pending trial.

In practice the difference between a city and a county prison was almost invisible. Dublin's size accounted for the presence, within a few kilometres of each other, of the city prison at Newgate and the county gaol at Gallows Hill in Kilmainham. Which prison convicted prisoners actually served their sentences in depended on where they were convicted.

Once the excitements of 1798 and 1803 were behind it, the new county gaol at Kilmainham settled down. The jailers or turnkeys brought with them from the old gaol many of the habits of extortion and bribery that had been a commanding feature of the old regime. Other prison officials followed suit. The culture changed somewhat as the 19th century progressed but it was often a case of two steps forward and one back.

A principal reason for this was that, right from the start, the new gaol failed to live up to the promise of the Howard reforms. The requirement for single-cell occupancy was met for only a short while in the early 1840s before facilities were overwhelmed by the Famine. A spike in crime, not least prostitution, followed the demobilisation of common soldiers at the end of the Napoleonic wars. There was overcrowding in the new prison from the very start.

A prison van arrives at Kilmainham, from the *Illustrated London News*, 1881.

It was all a good example of benign legislation only gradually coming to terms with a prevailing and engrained culture. None the less, things did improve, albeit slowly. The reforming legislation had provided for a new inspectorate, which was to visit every gaol in its catchment area at least once every two years. Kilmainham was inspected annually and there is evidence that the inspectors were extremely diligent in the exercise of their duties.

Another conspicuous part of Howard's reforms was an emphasis on personal improvement and redemption through religious observance. That was driven, from its English base, by low-church Protestantism and collateral movements like Methodism, whose founder – John Wesley – had paid no fewer than 21 evangelising visits to Ireland before his death in 1791. However, in Ireland, especially among the lower classes most likely to find themselves in trouble with the law, differences of language and religious allegiance proved stubbornly resistant to change or reform.

There was one other constant at Kilmainham, however, which is still there today. Over the doorway at the main entrance is a tympanum – a recessed space set in a pediment or doorway – showing five chained and shackled serpents with scaly bodies and dragons' or crocodiles' heads, each attacking the other. It is rather scary even today, and was certainly intended to put the fear of God into any inmate arriving at Kilmainham for the first time. No doubt it succeeded.

The Victorian London prison, Newgate. Prisoners in the exercise yard. Engraving by Gustave Doré and Blanchard Jerrold, 1872.

The Early 19th Century

Very gradually, as Britain and Ireland moved slowly towards the Victorian age, the desire for genuine reform and a new philosophy of prisons advanced. Just how urgent this nascent movement had become was demonstrated in an inspector's report on Kilmainham for the year 1809. He pointed out that no proper attempt was being made by the prison authorities to segregate ordinary criminals – many of them viciously malevolent – from criminals who suffered with mental illness. These poor souls were regarded simply as criminals like the rest of them. Astonishingly, segregation of these two groups was not completed until as late as the 1870s.

Then came misfortune. There was a fire in the gaol in 1817 which caused extensive damage to what is now the west wing – the east wing existed but not yet in its current form. The conflagration necessitated the rebuilding of the structure. The new design incorporated many features that were a substantial improvement on the old, not least in the provision of day rooms for prisoners, where they could be set to tasks and occupations that served some useful purpose, even if it was only to relieve the boredom of incarceration.

An 1825 report on county prisons ranked Kilmainham towards the bottom in comparative terms. Overcrowding was still a chronic difficulty in the prison and it may have been the case that the proper segregation of the sexes was either neglected or not entirely possible as yet. There is, however, some confusion with regard to this, for inspectors' reports for that period praise the running of the female prison over that of the male prison.

A further report, five years later in 1830, ranked Kilmainham among the four worst county prisons in Ireland. All these reports were themselves straws in the wind, evidence of a new sensibility regarding the superintendence and management

Prisoners with mental health difficulties formed part of the general population of Kilmainham Gaol until the late 19th century, when segregation was introduced.

of prisons in Britain and Ireland. The situation was changing from that which existed in the 18th century, when prisoners were incarcerated and the key figuratively thrown away. The state was now gradually inserting itself into the whole regime of dealing with crime and punishment.

The Irish Prisons Act of 1826 was indicative of this process. This piece of legislation was an assertion by the state that it was the ultimate controlling agent in the prison system and that the structures of management and superintendence that it proposed were to be the norm for the future. Moreover, the police were also reformed in order to complement this process. A city police force of sorts had existed in Dublin since 1786, the first of its kind in Britain or Ireland. By 1836, it was reconstituted as the Dublin Metropolitan Police (DMP), an unarmed civic police force, based on the model of the London Metropolitan Police that had been established by Sir Robert Peel – himself a former chief secretary of Ireland – seven years earlier.

In short, what was happening was a distinct movement of prison governance from private to state control. Jailers and turnkeys were no longer to be freelance opportunists, augmenting their miserable wages through extortion and fines. They were gradually being turned into civil servants. As ever, this was no overnight process – it did not happen just by throwing a switch or passing a bill in parliament – but there was no doubt at all about the overall direction of travel.

The Royal Irish Constabulary (RIC) was Ireland's major police force for most of the 19th and early 20th centuries. The Dublin Metropolitan Police controlled the capital. Derry and Belfast had special divisions within the RIC. In 1922 the RIC was replaced by two new police forces. The Garda Síochána (Guardians of the Peace) patrolled the Irish Free State (now the Republic of Ireland). The Royal Ulster Constabulary patrolled the Northern Ireland state, which remained in the UK.

Panopticon

In the 18th century, John Howard was the person most influential in introducing new ideas into the prison system. His ideas were adopted, albeit slowly and incompletely.

Jeremy Bentham.

However, in the 19th century, as the state became ever more assertive in the whole area of crime and punishment, it looked for a new philosophy to underpin its presence. It came from Jeremy Bentham (1748–1832), by some way the most influential British thinker of the age, at least in so far as his thought affected public policy. Bentham is most associated with that branch of philosophy known as utilitarianism, summed up in his famous formula that the object of public policy should be to secure the greatest happiness of the greatest number.

For prisons, he proposed what he called a Panopticon. This meant a prison design that afforded prison warders and authorities the greatest possible opportunity to observe their charges or, to put it in a rather more sinister formulation, to keep them under maximum surveillance for as much of the time as possible. According to this prescription for prison architecture, there was to be a central observation platform at the heart of the prison, with cells arranged all around it on a number of tiered floors in a series of semi-circles or ellipses.

As with all new proposals, this one took time to catch on. Conservatism and ingrained habits of old are a running theme in this story. Not all was new, however, for Bentham's scheme was predicated on the idea that the governor of such an institution could run it at his own personal profit – some 18th-century ideas carried over into the new thinking! Where to draw the line between private and state control is a consideration that persists even today.

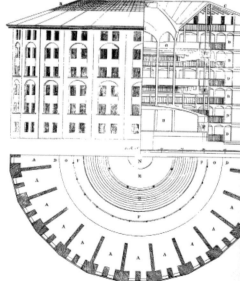

Design for a Panopticon prison.

Between 1788 and 1868, about 162,000 convicts were transported from Britain and Ireland to various penal colonies in Australia. The British government began transporting convicts overseas to American colonies in the early 18th century. Convicts in Sydney.

However, Bentham's proposals did eventually bear fruit, although this was cross-pollinated by other ideas. Among these ideas was a gradual retreat from Howard's humanitarianism towards a more severe and disciplined prison regime. Prisoners were closely monitored, but they were also robbed of their individual identities and were identified by a number rather than a name. There was a supervised work routine, with short breaks for meals and exercise – at which silence had to be observed.

The model for this new kind of prison opened at Pentonville in London in 1842. It was to be very influential when Kilmainham came to extend its footprint in the 1850s and 1860s by building the east wing. It was built on these reformed lines: indeed the best-known image of the entire prison is the central observation platform or main hall around which everything else radiates.

That was for the future. By the 1830s, there were still complaints that reports and proposals for reform were being ignored. More space was required to alleviate the chronic overcrowding, a problem exacerbated by the practice of housing convicts at Kilmainham prior to their transportation to the colonies. The prison was the transportation depot for the entire east coast of Ireland.

No set of reforms could have coped with what was coming next. Ireland was on the brink of the greatest social disaster in her history.

Convicts excercising at Pentonville Prison in London, chained together, with masks covering their faces.

The Gaol in 1840: A Review

A person born in 1770 would have attained the allotted biblical lifespan of three score years and 10 by 1840. In the context of Kilmainham Gaol, this affords an opportunity to take stock and to measure the enormous changes that had taken place in that notional lifetime.

Modern penology hardly existed in 1770, although the early writings of di Beccaria and Howard were beginning to have their slow – very slow – effect. The gaol was still the old one, down by the Camac and a short distance to the east of Gallows Hill. Its cells gave out onto the street and the wretched inmates could beg alms from passers-by in order to buy food or drink or bribe the turnkeys. The passage of goods in and out of prisons was a highly profitable business. Kilmainham old gaol was no exception to the observation that contemporary prisons were little more than exploitative hostels. Conditions, by common consent, were utterly wretched.

One of Howard's main recommendations was that, when it came time to build a new prison, it should be located on rising ground, to ensure better ventilation and circulation of air generally. He believed that this s was essential for the health of the prisoners. The site for the new prison at Gallows Hill was chosen accordingly. Construction work began in the 1780s and the new gaol was opened in 1796.

The whole process of prison reform in the 19th century entailed a movement from private to public provision. The old system had been run by wardens and turnkeys in their own material interests. The

A petty court session in Dublin, mid-19th century.

new system moved governance of prisons more and more into the public realm, regulated by parliamentary statute and ministerial order. Management of the system was no longer in the hands of those immediately present: it was now regulated remotely.

In Ireland, the period 1770 to 1840 – the life span of our imaginary person – was a time of upheaval and unprecedented population explosion. The 1798 rebellion ended the long 18th-century peace and ushered in the Act of Union. This legislation, which came into force on 1 January 1801, ended the old, local (and corrupt) Dublin parliament and made Ireland fully a part of the metropolitan British state. The Union was supposed to have been accompanied by Catholic Emancipation, as a quid pro quo. This would have removed all or most of the existing prohibitions on Catholics. King George III would not countenance this and so it did not happen.

It meant that the Union was seen, right from the start, as an exercise in bad faith. Gradually, campaigns in support of reform developed in Ireland. The guiding spirit in all these, especially from the 1820s on, was the titanic figure of Daniel O'Connell. Eventually, in 1829, the London government was forced to concede Emancipation, so great had been the populist mobilisation in Ireland in support of O'Connell. This triumph naturally entailed some breaches of repressive laws, all of which put pressure on the prison system.

Likewise, the Tithe War of the 1830s added more to the prison population. We cannot be sure how many people ended up in Kilmainham as a result of these agitations, but it would be naive to suppose that the number was zero.

The last elected parliament in Ireland, 1790, at College Green.

Early 1840s Reforms

Kilmainham came out towards the end of a comparative list of Irish county prisons in an 1825 report. The ever-present problem of overcrowding remained intractable, as did the inadequate regime for the separation of men and women. Five years later, a similar report produced a similar verdict: Kilmainham was among the four worst county jails in Ireland.

All through the 1830s, the tone of the reports became increasingly frustrated as recommendations for improvement were ignored or – just as likely – were incapable of being carried out for want of resources.

This latter point was at least addressed in 1840, when the Dublin grand jury – a body that was legislated out of existence the following year – made available the sum of £1,550 in order to provide an additional 30 cells for the exclusive accommodation of women. Moreover, a new prison was established in Smithfield, just west of the city centre but part of the city fabric, unlike suburban Kilmainham. This eased some of the worst pressure on Kilmainham.

Kilmainham was one of the first prisons in Ireland to respond to the new Pentonville architectural innovations in the form of the 1840s extension to the west wing. Joshua Jebb, the architect of Pentonville, was consulted on this refurbishment. Pentonville was transformative:

John Howard visiting a prison: a group of inmates sitting or lying on the floor. Etching by J. Hogg after F. Wheatley.

prisons that had upgraded or rebuilt to reflect current reform thinking found themselves out of date once the Pentonville system came along.

The reforms had a beneficial effect on ventilation, a central requirement of all prison reform movements. The three governing principles of Howard's reforms had been security, hygiene – ventilation was critical in this regard – and reformation. On that latter point, the prison chaplain was almost the co-equal of the prison governor in the day-to-day administration of a prison. That was in Great Britain; in Ireland, because of the religious divide, chaplains had a much tougher time of it.

The movement for prison reform in Britain was inevitably influential in Ireland. In Britain, there were a series of developments all pointing in the same direction. Millbank prison was opened in 1816, the first in the country for convicted prisoners, and the system of transportation to the remote colonies gradually began to weaken, although it was not abolished until the 1850s. Robert Peel's Prison Act of 1823 was the first of many reforming statutes enacted throughout the 19th century.

In the context of Kilmainham's modest reforms of 1840, the biggest influences were probably the American system of silence and separation, and the development of Pentonville. Indeed, a new Gaol Act passed in London in 1839 provided for solitary confinement, another incentive to try to sort out the overcrowding in Kilmainham once and for all.

These modest, crabbing reforms were at least carrying Kilmainham and the rest of the Irish prison system towards the light. Then came the Great Famine of 1845–52, which devastated the country. Of a population of eight million, a million died and a similar number emigrated. As always in such disasters, the heaviest blow fell upon the poorest, and it was they who now overwhelmed the prison system.

Attack on a potato store. Engraving from the *Illustrated London News,* 1842.

Famine

The Great Irish Famine was the last great subsistence crisis in Western Europe. Its effect on Irish society was utterly transformative. There was a pre-Famine Ireland and a post-Famine Ireland and they were very different places.

The cause of the disaster was the over-reliance on a single crop, the potato. When a mysterious potato blight devastated the crop in 1845 and in subsequent years, people – the poorest in particular – had little or nothing else to fall back on. Ireland starved.

The cause of the blight was not discovered until nearly 40 years later. As one distinguished historian of the Famine remarked, Ireland was desperately unlucky. The blight struck at a time of maximum population pressure – emigration schemes would almost certainly have relieved the pressure, as happened elsewhere – but before scientific analysis of the basic cause was available.

The London government did not do remotely enough to tackle the crisis, leaving everything to the workings of the market in a blatant case of ideological fanaticism triumphing over common sense and ordinary humanity. This belief in the benign hand of the free market, with which the government should not interfere, was a commonplace of the era.

Indeed, one of the most draconian measures proposed was the notorious Quarter Acre Clause of 1847, proposed in parliament by Sir William Gregory, later to be the husband of the more celebrated Lady Gregory of Literary Revival fame. The so-called 'Gregory Clause' stipulated that any tenant with a holding of more than a quarter of an acre must surrender it in perpetuity in order to be eligible for public relief. So, the choice was your cabin and its miserable holding, the only home you knew, or the horrors of the workhouse.

William Henry Gregory, parodied in *Vanity Fair*, 1871.

Peasants besieging a workhouse door.

In these circumstances of such widespread misery and destitution, it is hardly surprising that the prison population increased. Desperate people stole food. Those who were caught went to prison. Then, in an act foolish even by the standards of the government of the day, London passed a Vagrant Act, which meant that beggars – of whom, in the prevailing circumstances there was now a multitude – were criminalised and were flung in jail.

The inspector of Kilmainham produced a report for 1847 that bristled with outrage at the huge numbers of destitute paupers flung into the gaol. 'Numbers of these wretched creatures are obliged to lie on straw in the passages and dayrooms without a possibility of washing … '. Filthy, ragged and diseased, as many were, they introduced fever and dysentery into a prison already buckling under the influx of the poor. As early as 1846, the inspector recommended a change in the prison diet, given the failure of the potato crop. Until a few years earlier, the diet had been mainly meal, but this had been replaced by potatoes, not because they were more nutritious – although they were – but because they were cheaper. Henceforth, bread was to be the staple.

Many desperate people deliberately committed crimes in order to be committed to prisons like Kilmainham. The conditions and the food, wretched as they were, were superior to the workhouse. No prison system could have coped in similar circumstances, and Kilmainham was no exception. The price was very high: a prison designed for about 150 inmates held many more by 1850.

An Ejected Family, Erskine Nicol, 1825–1904.

Young Ireland and 1848

Daniel O'Connell.

Daniel O'Connell died, worn out, in 1847. He had been increasingly estranged from a younger, more radical faction in his movement who styled themselves as Young Ireland. They were cultural nationalists for the most part, but shot through with some of the residual republicanism of 1798. More immediately, they were under the influence of contemporary German thought, with its emphasis on the integrity of native culture, as that country reacted to the devastation wrought upon it by Napoleon.

Unlike the young cultural enthusiasts, O'Connell had been a utilitarian of the Bentham school. He cared little for the Irish language; the Young Irelanders cared for it a lot. These differences of emphasis were quickened by the Famine and drew ever more radical people to the Young Ireland cause.

Young Ireland also contained a significant number of idealistic Protestants, who naturally found O'Connell's emphasis on Catholic solidarity troubling. Prominent among these was William Smith O'Brien, an Anglican landlord from County Limerick, who became the official Young Ireland spokesman in parliament in 1847. He and O'Connell had always been at odds, and O'Connell's eldest son, John, held O'Brien in open contempt.

The growing unrest in Ireland met with a heavy-handed response from London. The government's hands-off approach to the Famine was not matched by its attitude to law and order. The Treason Felony Act of 1848 suspended habeas corpus.

Thomas Francis Meagher.

One of Smith O'Brien's closest associates was Thomas Francis Meagher, the son of a wealthy businessman from Waterford. Both were arrested and charged in early 1848 but acquitted. The ever heavier hand of the London authorities, together with the disaster of the Famine, led them to the view that a rising was inevitable.

The idea that this well-meaning group of idealists, writers and intellectuals could mobilise a revolutionary army in the desperate social conditions prevailing in the

William Smith O'Brien statue, O'Connell Street, Dublin.

famine-ridden Ireland of the 1840s was a ridiculous one. People were starving; they wanted food, not revolution. None the less, these matters are not always settled by logic, and an attempt of sorts did go ahead.

What followed was pathetic. The 'rising' was little more than an affray at the house of one Widow McCormack in Ballingarry, County Tipperary. Smith O'Brien had been trying unsuccessfully to raise insurgent troops in the area; the Catholic authorities were opposed to his efforts and the Royal Irish Constabulary (RIC) were on to him. When his small group realised that the RIC had occupied the Widow McCormack's house – with some child hostages – they attacked it. Two Young Irelanders died in the succeeding exchange of fire. All 46 RIC men and all the children were unharmed.

It was over before it began and was an embarrassing shambles. However, it was later elevated into the pantheon of successive Irish nationalist uprisings against England: this was amplified by Pádraig Pearse years later. In nation-making, myths are as important as facts – even more, at times.

After this debacle the leaders were arrested and Kilmainham Gaol became home to William Smith O'Brien and Thomas Francis Meagher.

The attack on Widow McCormack's house.

William Smith O'Brien

O'Brien is a common surname in Ireland, but William Smith O'Brien was the real thing, a lineal descendant of Brian Ború. These O'Briens had had a turbulent history down the centuries, tacking and veering with all prevailing winds. The senior male of the family was ennobled as Lord Inchiquin, a title to which William's elder brother succeeded in due course. Their family seat was the impressive medieval pile of Dromoland Castle in County Clare, and it was there that William Smith O'Brien was born in 1803.

He was educated at Harrow and qualified for the Bar but never practised. Instead, he found himself in parliament at 25, the member for his father's pocket borough of Ennis. This brought him into contact with Daniel O'Connell, soon to be the member for County Clare and the most notable man in Ireland. From the start, relations between the two were brittle.

Formally, Smith O'Brien supported O'Connell, although there was no warmth or affinity between them.

In the 1840s, he was drawn towards the Young Ireland movement. In particular, he supported the establishment of new universities on non-denominational lines – as did Young Ireland – although O'Connell and the Catholic hierarchy were opposed to what they called 'godless colleges'.

The O'Brien family had an estate at Cahermoyle, County Limerick. Smith O'Brien had inherited this, and its 5,000 acres gave him a gentlemanly living.

The arrest of William Smith O'Brien.

This was an improbable background for a revolutionary and in the events that followed, Smith O'Brien was somewhat reluctantly propelled to the fore. The French Revolution in early 1848 impressed him and his rhetoric became more urgent. He went to Paris, and although he denied accusations that he was seeking French military support for an Irish uprising, he was frustrated by British coercion laws and came to the view that some sort of insurrectionary challenge to British rule in Ireland was inevitable.

The support he was promised across the south of Ireland quickly vanished. The authorities were

The removal of Smith O'Brien to prison, under sentence of death.

on to him and the Catholic clergy were hostile to his manoeuvres. This culminated in the shambles at Ballingarry where, to his credit, he displayed singular physical courage in impossible circumstances. He negotiated an end to the affray with minimal loss of life.

None the less, he was tried for and convicted of high treason, which is what landed him in Kilmainham. Sentenced to death, he was instead transported to Tasmania and released in 1854. He returned to Europe, travelled widely and did not resume an active political career. He did, however, remain a severe critic of British rule in Ireland.

William Smith O'Brien's journey to Kilmainham Gaol may have been an improbable one but it was important in terms of the history of the prison. Kilmainham's claim to fame rests almost entirely upon the succession of nationalist and republican prisoners who were held there and who died there. Smith O'Brien now joined the apostolic succession of heroes – from Henry Joy McCracken, the Sheares brothers, Robert Emmet and Thomas Russell – while being a key link in a tradition that was to culminate in the executions following the 1916 Rising.

Smith O'Brien's cottage in Port Arthur, Tasmania.

Thomas Francis Meagher

Thomas Francis Meagher (1823–1867) was the other 1848 link in the chain that marked out Kilmainham Gaol's place in Irish history. From that notable and prosperous Catholic merchant class of the south-east, Meagher was born in Waterford, the son of a ship owner. This monied class in the south-east was a crucial element in the early formation of Irish Catholic nationalism, providing social leadership and the prestige that money brings. Meagher was educated at Clongowes Wood College in County Kildare – the first Jesuit school established in Britain or Ireland since the Reformation – and later at Stonyhurst College in Lancashire, another Jesuit school. It was an elite formation.

Returning to Ireland, he formed friendships with men influential in the Young Ireland movement, especially Thomas Davis and Charles Gavan Duffy. He also knew William Smith O'Brien and the radical John Mitchel. This drew him more and more into the orbit of this group, whose principal marker of difference with Daniel O'Connell was their cultural nationalism and their refusal to rule out armed force in support of nationalist ambitions.

Meagher crystallised this issue in an address that secured him his place in history. On 28 July 1846, in a speech in Conciliation Hall,

Dublin, he refused to 'renounce the sword' as a revolutionary tactic; he used the imagery of the sword eight times in all in that speech. The novelist William Makepeace Thackeray subsequently dubbed him 'Meagher of the Sword'. The name stuck.

Meagher's other claim to fame is still very much with us. In April 1848, he went to Paris, then seething in the wake of the February revolution that ended the reign of Louis-Philippe and restored republican government, at least for a few years until Louis Napoleon's *coup d'état* ushered in the Second Empire. From Paris, Meagher returned to Ireland bearing an Irish version of the French revolutionary tricolour. Instead of blue, white and red, its colours were green, white and orange, symbolising the white of peace standing between the nationalist green and the unionist orange. It is today the national flag of the Republic of Ireland.

Thomas Francis Meagher.

Meagher was one of William Smith O'Brien's principal lieutenants in the run-up to the affray at Ballingarry in 1848. He went on a recruiting drive in the south-east but was arrested and released on bail. When the planned uprising did take place at the Widow McCormack's, Meagher was not present. This did not stop the authorities from charging him with high treason.

Thus, he too made his way to Kilmainham.

William Smith O'Brien, seated, and Thomas Francis Meagher flanked by a prison guard and jailer at Kilmainham Gaol, Dublin, 1848, before being deported to Tasmania.

Like Smith O'Brien, Meagher was transported to Tasmania, from where he escaped and made his way to the United States. There, he distinguished himself as a general in the Union army during the Civil War and ended up as acting governor of Montana, not yet a state. A controversial figure, he died in murky and mysterious circumstances, with foul play suspected.

General Meagher at the Battle of Fair Oaks, Virginia,1 June 1862.

The East Wing

All the old, intractable problems of Kilmainham persisted into the 1850s. In Britain, about 25 per cent of prisoners were women; in Ireland, the figure was 50 per cent. Successive inspectors' reports pointed out the prison's chronic shortcomings, but change came very slowly. Ireland was prostrate, reeling from the catastrophe of the Great Famine. However, the urge for reform and improvement, so much a feature of the High Victorian noonday, made itself felt eventually, even in the prison environment.

The immediate pretext for building a new wing at Kilmainham was to solve the segregation question once and for all. It was regarded as a scandal in Victorian times that the sexes were promiscuously mixed. That said, there had been progress; even during the Famine, it was not mentioned as an ongoing problem, so it can be inferred that the drift was in the right direction. In 1856, the decision was taken to build a second wing, one of whose principal functions was to be the accommodation of female prisoners, segregated at last from the men.

It took more than six years to build the east wing. The architect was John McCurdy, who adhered to the new vogue for prison design of which Pentonville in London was the exemplar. The principle of observation by the prison authorities resulted in the inclusion of the central viewing platform from which the warders could at all times see the individual cells ranged in three tiers around this central area. Moreover, every cell door had a spyhole through which each prisoner could be individually observed from time to time, as occasion demanded.

John Howard, Jeremy Bentham and other prison reformers, while not in agreement on every detail, were broadly in agreement on the more important ones. These were: confinement in individual cells at night; isolation of identifiable groups, as women, felons, prisoners suffering with mental illness and those guilty only of misdemeanours; and round-the-clock seclusion of individual prisoners. Bentham wished prisons to be laboratories in social engineering, leading to prisoner reform.

Drawing by Willey Reveley of a Panopticon prison, c. 1791, showing a cross section of the cells (H) and a skylight (M) to provide light and ventilation.

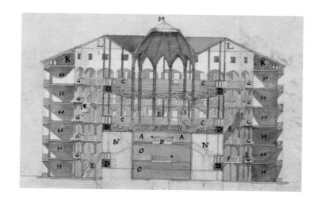

The other governing principles were solitude and silence and the hope that these would lead prisoners to self-contemplation leading to self-reform. In that connection, it was hoped that bible-reading would facilitate the process. This proved to be hopelessly idealistic, not least because of the old religious divide: most prisoners were Catholics, habituated to the idea that bible-reading was a Protestant fetish.

The new wing, which opened in stages in the early years of the 1860s, was flooded with light, for this too was part of the Victorian grand plan. The principal source of light was the splendid glass canopy that formed the roof of the east wing, but each cell had also been provided with a generous allowance of natural light. Only the punishment cells, reserved for the most recalcitrant and intractable prisoners, were devoid of light. These wretches could spend 14 days in those basement dungeons subsisting on bread and water. There was a limit to high-minded mid-Victorian idealism – and patience.

After all that, the women were indeed segregated – but not as the original intention dictated. They were left behind in the less appealing and gloomy west wing while the men were transferred to the relative luxury of the new east wing.

Inscription on the wall
of a cell at Kilmainham.

The Fenians

The Fenian Brotherhood, or Irish Republican Brotherhood (IRB), was founded jointly in Dublin and New York in 1858. Its prime mover in Ireland was James Stephens, a veteran of 1848 – he had been at Ballingarry – who had subsequently gone to France. While in Paris, he mixed in revolutionary circles, repatriating some of their conspiratorial techniques when he returned to Ireland.

James Stephens.

The Fenians represented a distinct change in the personality of Irish nationalism. While it still possessed that republican streak, drawing on the legacy of 1798 and 1848, its membership base was socially wider than before, less dominated by people like Smith O'Brien and Meagher, with their elite schooling and background. Moreover, that co-foundation in New York was hugely significant, mobilising Irish-American opinion in an Irish cause for the first time. The founding spirit there was John O'Mahony, another 1848 veteran. The Irish diaspora incubated a burning hatred of England over its shameful passivity during the Famine. This found expression in one of the Fenians' core principles: it was an out-and-out revolutionary movement. Having no truck with the prevarications and compromises of politics, its aim was to drive England out of Ireland by force of arms.

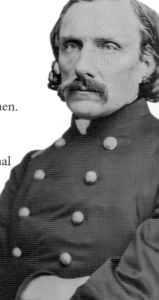

John O'Mahony in US army uniform.

The basic structural feature that Stephens brought back from the Paris secret societies was this: there was a local leader, known as a centre; each centre chose nine captains, each of whom chose nine sergeants, each of whom chose nine men. Information was passed to each rank on a need-to-know basis only. Within a few years, Stephens had tramped the country and established a national network based on this cell structure.

This revolutionary structure brought the Fenians into collision with the Catholic Church, which loathed secret societies. Not only did it regard them as godless, it had been a similar society that had chased the pope out of Rome in 1848. A distressed witness to that event had been Paul Cullen, then rector of the Irish College, now archbishop of Dublin, soon to be the first Irish cardinal, and by far the most substantial personality in the Irish hierarchy.

Attack on the prison van at Manchester, and rescue of the Fenian Leaders.

Cullen was no friend of the Protestant British state but he preferred it to what the Church regarded as a godless conspiracy against the established order. Cullen was alarmed by Stephens's success in mobilising so much of Ireland for the Fenian cause. He was right to be, for Stephens had charisma.

However, success can be its own worst enemy. Cell structure or no, the police were soon on to the Fenians. In 1865 Stephens and other leaders were arrested; they had been planning a rising, hoping to exploit the services of Irish-Americans now being demobilised at the end of the American Civil War. The Fenians never recovered from this pre-emptive strike. Belatedly, in 1867, they tripped off a feeble rising that was easily put down.

Fenianism was now a sleeping volcano. The Fenians remained a feature of Irish life, although as the decades passed they seemed ever more like yesterday's men. They were not; for without the Fenians, there would have been no 1916 Rising and the history of Ireland – and of Kilmainham Gaol – would have been very different.

Cardinal Cullen by an unknown artist.

Fenians Passing Through

James Stephens was among those lifted in 1865. He did not see the inside of Kilmainham Gaol because he was held less than a mile away in Richmond Prison, from which he soon managed to escape. Hundreds of Fenians were held in Kilmainham in the 1860s, confirming ever more its central place in the history and mythology of Irish republicanism. Kilmainham was deliberately chosen to house the Fenians after Stephens's escape from Richmond. The prison building was also deliberately strengthened to prevent further escapes.

John O'Leary was among the Fenian prisoners. Another veteran of Ballingarry in 1848, he was held in Kilmainham before being transferred to prison in England, where he served nine years of a twenty-year sentence. When he eventually returned to Ireland in the 1880s, his unrepentant Fenianism made him popular with a younger generation, none more so than W. B. Yeats, to whom O'Leary uttered the famous formula that in Ireland a man must have either the [Catholic] Church or the Fenians on his side.

Also in Kilmainham in the 1860s were others who were to be influential in the years ahead. Charles J. Kickham was from County Tipperary, a cousin of John O'Mahony. He had been a supporter of

Portrait of John O'Leary (1830–1907), Nationalist and Journalist, by John Butler Yeats.

various advanced nationalist causes since the 1840s, but his claim to fame rested on the pen, not the sword. In 1873, he published a novel, *Knocknagow: or The Homes of Tipperary*. It was a sentimental account of the virtuous rural life, in which most of the virtue was concentrated in the tenant farmers who were its principal protagonists. Its sentimentality earned it many sneers in later years but it had a powerful effect on late 19th-century nationalist consciousness, portraying ordinary people as social role models and repositories of courage, decency and self-reliance. The book has seldom, if ever, been out of print since its first publication.

Charles Joseph Kickham (9 May 1828–22 August 1882), Irish patriot, novelist and poet and founding member of the Irish Republican Brotherhood.

Another Fenian who saw the inside of Kilmainham was John Devoy, who was there in February 1867, although for how long is unclear. Devoy spent most of his life in America, having served five years in an English prison. He was released early – the original sentence had been 15 years' penal servitude – on condition that he never return to the United Kingdom. So he crossed the Atlantic, there to become the single most influential figure in Irish-American republican politics over two generations. His hand was across everything, from Parnell's new departure to the Land League to the 1916 Rising and beyond. He raised money for the cause back home, controlled as far as he could the perennially fractious nationalist support movements, and eventually supported the Anglo-Irish Treaty of 1921. He kept his promise not to return to the UK, but he lived long enough to visit an independent Ireland in 1924, where he was received with every honour.

James Devoy.

These were but a few of the hundreds of Fenians who passed through Kilmainham Gaol in the 1860s. Most of them are known to us thanks to the prison registers. The steady association between the gaol and republicanism – which is what gives Kilmainham its place in history – was growing ever stronger.

O'Donovan Rossa

Of all the Fenians who passed through Kilmainham in the 1860s, few had as colourful a subsequent career, or as richly a symbolic one, as Jeremiah O'Donovan Rossa. He had a long life, from 1831 to 1915. He founded a political and literary society in his native West Cork in 1856; two years later, it was folded into the IRB. His native place was Rosscarberry and it was from there that he took his surname suffix, a name that is still a common male forename in Ireland.

His early Fenian activities in his locality included drilling and other public displays, which inevitably drew the attention of the police – helped by a priest who informed on O'Donovan Rossa, probably breaking the seal of the confessional in the process, for that seems to have been the source of his intelligence. O'Donovan Rossa found himself in jail – whether in Kilmainham or elsewhere is uncertain, although more likely it was some prison nearer home.

After a few years in the United States, he returned to Ireland and became business manager of the *Irish People*, the Fenian newspaper. He was caught in the pre-emptive round-up and tried before the notorious Judge William Keogh, a former nationalist who had turned his coat quite spectacularly. It was at this point that O'Donovan Rossa passed through Kilmainham, having been instrumental in helping James Stephens escape from Richmond Prison.

At his trial, Rossa realised the inevitability of conviction and spent as much of the time as he could guying Keogh and generally putting on a performance. He lit into Keogh in a closing address lasting eight

Four of the five Fenian prisoners (John Devoy was the fifth).

The five Fenian prisoners who were released by the British to the United States in 1871, and were shipped together aboard the *Cuba*.

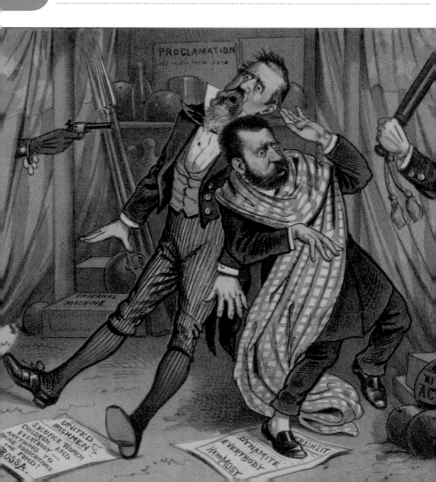

hours. When the wretched judge eventually got a word in, it was to sentence Rossa to life imprisonment. He spent the next few years in a number of English prisons, in one of which he found himself with John Devoy. Like Devoy, he got an early release in 1871, but not before suffering some cruel and degrading treatment.

He went back to the United States, where he had an erratic business career while succeeding John O'Mahony, who had died, as head of the American Fenians. O'Donovan Rossa then proposed what he called a 'skirmishing fund' to finance a series of bomb attacks in British cities. Devoy, whose influence was increasing by the day, was opposed to this. Although O'Donovan Rossa's stock fell as Devoy's rose, the skirmishing fund produced a sporadic series of bomb attacks in Britain in the first half of the 1880s. Among the targets were the Underground railway, Great Scotland Yard and the Tower of London. They even got a bomb to explode in the chamber of the House of Commons.

After that, O'Donovan Rossa does not quite disappear from history but the story of his later years is of little account. He died in New York in 1915 and his body was returned to Ireland. At his graveside, Pádraig Pearse, soon to be the formal leader of the 1916 Rising, gave the graveside oration – one of the greatest speeches in Irish history – in which he located Jeremiah O'Donovan Rossa seamlessly in the apostolic tradition of militant Irish republicanism.

Jeremiah O'Donovan Rossa featuring in an American satrical cartoon of 1885.

Parnell

Charles Stewart Parnell was an unlikely leader of Irish nationalism. A Protestant landed gentleman from County Wicklow, he was a poor public speaker and had a superstitious hatred of the colour green. Nevertheless, he found himself in the House of Commons at the age of 27. He attached himself to a group of genteel Irish members whose ambition was to gain a degree of Irish autonomy within a federal UK system: home rule.

Charles Stewart Parnell.

For Parnell, this parliamentary group was far too genteel and polite for its own good. Although he was a born leader, he himself was aloof and remote, caring little either for convention or what others thought of him. He had no illusions about the English, whom he disliked and of whom he said on one occasion that 'we will never gain anything from [her] unless we tread upon her toes – we will never gain a single sixpenny-worth by conciliation.'

This drew him to a group within the home rulers who believed in more robust parliamentary tactics. They filibustered legislation by talking it out endlessly in an attempt to frustrate the entire business of the house. At the time, there was no provision under house rules to foreclose a debate. This was treading on English toes with a vengeance and Parnell soon emerged as leader of this group.

This radicalism drew him close to other radicals, not least those agitating for tenant rights in the impoverished west. In 1879, he became the inaugural leader of the Land League, a national coalition seeking the establishment of a peasant proprietary. Even more sensationally, he now formed an alliance with Fenians – hitherto inimical to all forms of parliamentary politics – and this effectively united all the forces within Irish nationalism and gave them tremendous momentum. At the head of this mass movement, and its unquestioned leader in parliament, was Parnell.

Parnell addressing a meeting.

The immediate result was the Land Act of 1881, which conceded the Land League's headline demands and established a Land Commission to adjudicate on fair rents. Parnell, who had been arrested in October 1881 on a charge of incitement, and was being held in Kilmainham, rejected the legislation as insufficient. In the gaol, Parnell was accommodated in some comfort; many ordinary prisoners were transferred to Grangegorman to make room for the great man.

Even though Parnell was in Kilmainham, Ireland did not quieten down and agrarian protest threatened to run out of control. 'Captain Moonlight', a generic term for agrarian secret societies, not squeamish about violence or even murder, made his terrifying appearance. It seemed that the only thing worse than having Parnell out and about was having him in jail, so Prime Minister Gladstone proposed a deal.

Parnell addressing an anti-rent meeting at Limerick, 1879.

Captain William O'Shea and his wife, Katharine.

The Kilmainham Treaty

The deal, known ever after as the Kilmainham Treaty, was the product of six months of secret negotiations between intermediaries acting under Gladstone's instructions and Parnell in Kilmainham. Gladstone was anxious to damp down the fires that blazed in Ireland. Parnell wanted out for personal reasons: he had begun an affair with Katharine O'Shea, the wife of one of his MPs, and he wished to be with her, not least because their first child had just died.

Parnell wrote to Gladstone, stating that if tenants in arrears were embraced within the terms of the Land Act, he would support it and would use his influence to quell any further agrarian unrest. In addition, he wanted leaseholders – then excluded from the terms of the Act – to be included in its remit.

For each of the principals, it was a gamble. They both needed a deal, but it could not be formalised. It was, in effect, a gentleman's agreement, and therefore based on trust. The deal was done, Parnell and others imprisoned with him were released, and each man kept his side of the bargain. The Land Act was passed; Parnell began to wind up the Land League and now concentrated all his political energies on home rule. The 'treaty' was the whole basis of that trust between Gladstone and Parnell that lasted through the 1880s and foundered only in the shadow of the O'Shea divorce scandal.

It also marked the alliance between the Irish Party and the Liberals which lasted – with one small exception in 1885 – until the First World War. Thus the whole political context in which the vexed Irish question was to be addressed was set by this informal arrangement. It was a deal that survived all of its protagonists and was still the tacit underpinning of relationships as late as the Third Home Rule bill of 1914, negotiated by John Redmond, Parnell's successor as Irish leader, and H. H. Asquith, Gladstone's successor as PM.

In the end, the divorce crisis was fatal to Parnell. He had been living for years with Katharine

Gladstone at the despatch box in the Houses of Parliament, London.

Parnell in a
contemporary
drawing.

O'Shea, the wife of Captain William O'Shea MP, who eventually sought a divorce and named Parnell as co-respondent. When the party split in 1890, it was effectively asked to make a choice between Parnell continuing as leader or the Liberal alliance. Gladstone, under pressure from his many nonconformist members whose moral sensibilities were outraged by Parnell's adultery, had made it clear that the alliance was to be ended if the party continued with Parnell. In one of the most searing choices ever made by Irish politicians, they chose the Liberals over Parnell, thus precipitating one of the bitterest splits in Irish history.

It finished the great man. Within a year, Parnell was dead. He had fought three bitter by-elections, vainly trying to recover his lost position. At one of these, he was drenched to the skin in torrential weather. Never physically robust, he made his way back to Katharine in Brighton where he died. He was 45 years old.

Kilmainham Gaol main hall.

The Invincibles

The Invincibles were a maverick, freelance group of Fenian radicals. The heightened tensions aroused by the Land League agitation had provided a fertile context for radicalism. Many of this group had been active in the Land League but it had no formal connection with either the League or the IRB. It was founded in December 1881 and it was, from the beginning, set upon the assassination of key figures in the British administration in Ireland.

James Carey (1837-1883), by an unknown engraver, 1883.

In this ambition, they anticipated Michael Collins's Squad by 40 years, although they were vastly less effective. However, by the time Collins was setting up the Squad, the whole atmosphere of revolutionary Ireland had been transformed by the First World War and the 1916 Rising.

The Invincibles targeted in particular Superintendent John Mallon of the G Division of the Dublin Metropolitan Police. This division was responsible for intelligence-gathering on nationalist radicals – he was a spymaster. Mallon was the chief pair of eyes protecting the flank of British rule in Ireland. The Invincibles did not get him.

They also targeted the chief secretary of Ireland – the London cabinet minister with responsibility for the smaller island – who was no less a figure than W. E. Forster. William Edward Forster was a classic English Liberal, a Quaker who had married the daughter of Thomas Arnold, the famous public school headmaster, making him the brother-in-law of Matthew Arnold, the poet and cultural critic.

Forster was therefore a pillar of the mid-Victorian English establishment. His landmark Education Act of 1870, known ever after as Forster's Act, was regarded as one of the great reforming pieces of legislation. It made elementary education free and compulsory and stood at the head of a long process by which the British state gradually took education out of the hands of private providers and made it a public good.

That was in Gladstone's first government of 1868–74. The second Gladstone administration was

William Edward Forster caricatured in *Vanity Fair*, 1859.

formed six years later, in 1880, and Forster was sent to Ireland as chief secretary. A liberal lion in Britain, he had a transformation in Ireland. Horrified at the unrest in the country, he quickly became a severe law-and-order man, not the first Englishman to make that transition. Favouring coercion, he encouraged the police to fire on agitators, which earned him the sobriquet 'Buckshot Forster'. During the period of coercion preceding the Kilmainham Treaty, he oversaw the arrest and imprisonment of more than 900 members of the Land League.

The Invincibles did not get Forster, either. Disgusted by the Kilmainham Treaty and what he regarded, correctly, as a policy of conciliation towards Parnell, he resigned before the Invincibles could despatch him. However, they did get his successor.

The Invincibles made only one mark on Irish history, but it was an indelible one. Their day of destiny was 6 May 1882, just a few weeks after the conclusion of the Kilmainham Treaty. Coming so soon after Parnell's release, the horror of the Phoenix Park murders seemed to throw the whole question of law and order in Ireland back into the melting pot and fuelled the suspicion that Parnell himself had been part of the conspiracy.

The Invincibles had set out to murder Thomas Burke here seen being attacked, but also killed Cavendish who is lying in the foreground of this contemporary engraving.

The Phoenix Park Murders

Forster's successor as chief secretary was Lord Frederick Cavendish, born to the purple of the Devonshire ducal family. He was the younger brother of Lord Hartington, a key member of Gladstone's cabinet and later to be Duke of Devonshire. Cavendish was married to Gladstone's favourite niece. On the morning of 6 May, Cavendish had been sworn in as Forster's successor at Dublin Castle. He had then spent most of the day in discussions with the under-secretary, Thomas Henry Burke.

Lord Frederick Cavendish (1836–1882), English Liberal politician and Chief Secretary for Ireland in 1882.

The under-secretary was the head of the Irish domestic civil service. He was a Catholic, originally from County Galway, and had been a robust supporter of the policy of coercion driven by Forster. Now there was a new conciliatory dispensation because of the Kilmainham Treaty, so Burke and Cavendish had much to talk about.

They had an invitation to dine that evening with the Lord Lieutenant, Lord Spenser, at the Vice-Regal

Lodge in the Phoenix Park. Burke and Cavendish took advantage of the pleasant early summer day to walk from the Castle to the Lodge. Spenser, looking out for them, saw what he took to be a fistfight of sorts on the main drive through the Park. In fact, what he saw was the Phoenix Park Murders.

The Invincibles hardly knew who Cavendish was but they knew all about Burke, the law-and-order Catholic, and hated him accordingly. It was Burke they were after. Cavendish was collateral damage. Seven assassins formed three groups, all waiting for Burke and Cavendish further up the main road. They then walked towards the pair in their groups. Daniel Curley, Joe Hanlon and Michael Fagan formed the first group, Joe Brady and Tim Kelly were in the middle and Patrick Delaney and Thomas Caffrey brought up the rear. They had surgical knives and guns concealed about their persons.

It appears that Joe Brady did most of the killing, allowing the victims to pass before turning around and stabbing Burke in the back. Cavendish offered minimal resistance and he too was despatched.

Thomas Henry Burke (1829–1882). Permanent Under-Secretary at Dublin Castle, killed in Phoenix Park, 1882.

Before leaving, Brady used his surgeon's knife to cut Burke's throat.

Moreover, the group got clean away, one half believed to have been driven off north by a jarvey called James Fitzharris, universally known as 'Skin-the-Goat', the other half south in a cab driven by James Kavanagh, who later testified against his former comrades. Eventually, one of their number – not one of the murderers – also turned police informer. Brady and the others were arrested and charged with murder. It was no open-and-shut case. It required some very dubious testimony from informers, in particular the former Invincible James Carey, to secure convictions. Brady, Curley, Fagan, Kelly and Caffrey were hanged in Kilmainham. The other two were spared the gallows but were given long prison sentences.

Carey, the informer, was spirited away by the authorities to South Africa, along with his family. Sailing with them on board the *Melrose Castle*,

Joseph Brady being sentenced to death in April 1883, in a court sketch from the *Illustrated London News*.

bound for Cape Town, was one Patrick O'Donnell
from County Donegal. He was the Invincibles'
agent of revenge. As they neared their destination,
O'Donnell shot Carey and killed him. He himself
was hanged for this crime, although few Irish shed
any tears for Carey.

The surrender of
Patrick O'Donnell.

Other Nationalist Prisoners

Kilmainham Gaol did not just hold Parnell for six months in comfortable captivity. Many of his followers and supporters, including men of consequence, were also imprisoned there. For a while, it became a forcing house for nationalist talent, a finishing school of sorts. This reinforced its position, by now well established, as a sort of Irish patriotic academy. In this, it anticipated Frongoch in North Wales, a prison camp in which many of the leaders of the 1916 Rising were incarcerated and which, like Kilmainham Gaol in the early 1880s, quickened the pulses and the intellects of the nationalist leadership.

Of the men imprisoned with Parnell, none was of more significance – either then or in the future – than John Dillon. He was the second son of John Blake Dillon from County Roscommon, himself a veteran of the politics of the 1840s and one of the founders of the hugely influential *Nation* newspaper. The Dillons were upper-class Catholics; John Blake Dillon was a lawyer as well as having business interests back in County Roscommon.

John Dillon, his son, qualified in both medicine and law but was drawn to politics, influenced by his father's radicalism and that of his surviving companions from the excitements of the 1840s. Although not a Fenian, he admired their audacity and energy. He threw himself into the land war and was a close colleague of Parnell. It was for his activities in this endeavour that he was caught in the government round-up and lodged in Kilmainham.

Subsequently, Dillon entered parliament in the mid-1880s, took the anti-Parnell side at the time of the split and became deputy leader to John Redmond when the party re-united in 1900. He succeeded Redmond on the latter's death in 1918 – the last leader of Parnell's party – but by then Ireland was transformed and Dillon was yesterday's man.

In the 1880s, he had been very much today's man. So too was James J. O'Kelly, veteran of the French Foreign Legion and a former member of the supreme council of the IRB. There was a clear pattern of either sympathy for or actual membership of the Fenians among many of Parnell's chief lieutenants. O'Kelly was one of those who negotiated the New Departure in 1879.

John Dillon, MP for Tipperary.

He entered parliament, and soon afterwards he entered Kilmainham with Parnell and the others.

Among those he found there was Thomas Sexton from Waterford. He had been elected an MP in 1880 and was an enthusiastic proponent of obstruction and filibustering. A noted orator, he later held the House of Commons spellbound with his speech in support of the 1886 Home Rule bill. He went on to be a notable figure in Irish political life, twice lord mayor of Dublin and a director – and later chairman – of the *Freeman's Journal*, the leading nationalist newspaper of the day.

He lived long, dying at 85 in 1932. By then, his generation had been eclipsed by the revolutionary times that followed 1916. Still, they had represented a key link in the chain of Irish nationalism, and they were most of them graduates of Kilmainham Gaol.

An old engraving showing James Joseph O'Kelly (1845–1916), Irish nationalist (Fenian) journalist and British MP. O'Kelly arranged a prohibited meeting between Clan na Gael's William Carroll and Irish parliamentarians in a field at Brookeborough, County Fermanagh. This picture shows O'Kelly being ordered out of the field by a magistrate with the support of armed soldiers.

Ordinary Decent Criminals

Kilmainham Gaol holds its place in history because of its long association with leading figures in the Irish nationalist and republican traditions. Of course, the supreme moment of this tradition was to come in 1916. However, it is worth remembering that Kilmainham was built as an ordinary county prison, like the many others all across Ireland that most people would struggle to name. In addition, its normal stock-in-trade down the years were not people whose names have come down to us, hallowed in the national memory. Most of them were just ordinary criminals, of which Dublin and its environs never had any shortage. We even know the names of these 'ordinary' criminals, thanks to the prison registers.

That said, it is easy to caricature and exaggerate. In the period immediately before the 1916 Rising, the number of indictable offences committed in the metropolitan police district, covering the city proper and the suburbs, averaged only about 3,000 a year. Most of these were minor offences against property, misdemeanours rather than felonies, of which there were relatively few. Even allowing for the under-reporting of some crimes, especially in the domestic sphere, Dublin was not a notably crime-ridden city, although it was a conspicuously poor one.

People waiting to see prisoners at Kilmainham in 1881.

Of the cases coming before the Dublin magistrates around the turn of the century, about a third involved either assault or drunkenness or both. Prostitution was a perennial problem, ubiquitous as it was with so many British military housed in local barracks and concentrated in the notorious Monto red light district, bang in the city centre just to the north of Sackville Street, and immortalised by Joyce in *Ulysses*. Dublin consistently recorded greater numbers of prostitutes in the late 19th century than did comparable British cities.

In the decades following the building of Kilmainham's east wing, the number of criminal convictions in Dublin – and consequently the numbers imprisoned in Kilmainham or anywhere else – fell steadily, despite all the excitements of the Parnell years. None the less, they did not disappear. Those who were imprisoned were generally sent either to Mountjoy, which had replaced Newgate in 1850, or Kilmainham. Most sentences were short and the regime comprised the normal practices of the time for prisoners: Sewing mailbags, breaking stones or – most detested of all – oakum picking. Oakum was a fibrous material infused with tar, used for all kinds of sealing, including on board ship. It was horrible stuff. There was also a two-hour shift on the crank pump, which had been a feature of Kilmainham since 1862.

In effect, Kilmainham became a hard labour prison, even for those serving short sentences, in the latter part of the 19th century, before closing as a prison facility in 1910. The hard labour of breaking stones, performed by so many men, took place in the prison yard that would carry the story of the prison to its apotheosis. It was here, in the stonebreakers' yard at Kilmainham, that 14 of the leaders of the 1916 Rising were executed.

The stonebreakers' yard at Kilmainham, 1881.

The 1916 Rising

If the rising had not happened the history of Ireland would have been very different. Likewise, this little history would have been only half the length it is, and there may have been no requirement for a history at all. At first, after the Civil War of 1922–23, Kilmainham was associated with the bitterness of that conflict and allowed to fall into disregarded neglect. By 1960, however, the mood had changed. Kilmainham became a sacred shrine to commemorate the sacrifices of the 1916 leaders. It is the reason visitors flock to it today.

The rising began on Easter Monday and lasted until the surrender on the following Saturday afternoon. The members of the Irish Volunteers and the Irish Citizen Army who were now under arrest were dispersed throughout the Dublin prison system. After the surrender, the rebels were in the hands of General Sir John Maxwell, the supreme military commander of British troops in Ireland since the previous Wednesday. He arrived in Dublin on the Friday, with the rising on the point of military collapse. Maxwell was in his 50s, a career officer of no great distinction. His instructions were an invitation to disaster: he could take 'all such measures as may in his opinion' be necessary.

Maxwell was thus given a free hand – the words were explicitly used in his instructions. In effect, British politicians were abdicating any responsibility for the response to the rising and leaving it to a military man of minimal distinction and one, moreover, who had in the past expressed some very disobliging views about the Irish.

A montage of the leaders of the 1916 Rising executed by the British. Tom Clarke is seated in the centre and Seán Mac Diarmada is to his right shoulder.

When Kilmainham was closed in 1910 it became a military detention barracks, and that is why it was the main centre for processing the military legal cases against the rebels.

Sixteen men died. Fourteen were executed by firing squad in the stonebreakers' yard in Kilmainham; one, Thomas Kent, was shot in Cork, and one, Roger Casement, was hanged in London. These executions began the change in Irish public opinion, which had at first been generally hostile to the rising. The novelist James Stephens, whose diary of the rising is the most acute contemporary account, wrote: 'Ireland is not cowed … she was not with the revolution, but in a few months she will be, and her heart which was withering will be warmed by the knowledge that men have thought her worth dying for.'

Other contemporaries agreed, not awaiting the benefits of hindsight. In the House of Commons, John Dillon immediately denounced the executions. Bernard Shaw pointed out their folly. One English writer, contemplating the executions years later, wrote simply: 'It was reasonable justice to shoot after trial people who had started an armed rebellion during a war, but it was unimaginably stupid politics.'

The scene of the executions at Kilmainham in 1916.

Pádraig Pearse

Pádraig Pearse was the great icon of the rising. It was his image, more than any other, that was reverentially displayed in homes all over Ireland in the generations that followed.

Pádraig Pearse.

He was first and foremost an Irish-language enthusiast and teacher. A natural writer and communicator, he edited the official newspaper of the Gaelic League for a number of years. He was also an educationalist – and a very enlightened one, placing the emphasis on what we would now call child-centred concerns at a time when the prevailing authoritarian ethic still held sway in most schools. His school, St Enda's, in Dublin, was steeped in the promotion of Gaelic culture. Many of its alumni went on to play important roles in an independent Ireland, and most of them remembered their martyred teacher with gratitude and affection.

Inevitably, all this cultural swirl drew Pearse towards the radical end of nationalist politics. That said, he did not really come to this position until late in the day. He had been relatively moderate in his political allegiances for most of the opening decade of the 20th century, but was gradually drawn to the more urgent nationalism of the IRB/Fenians, into which body he was inducted in late 1913. He was a founder member of the Irish Volunteers.

Pearse making a public declaration.

He went to the United States in early 1914 to raise money both for the Volunteers and for St Enda's, where he was constantly under financial pressure. This brought him into contact with leading republican supporters there, especially John Devoy and the influential Joe McGarrity. When the First World War started, the Volunteers split; Pearse took the more radical side which retained the existing name.

When Pádraig Pearse asked Tom Clarke how impassioned the speech should be, Clarke replied: 'Make it hot as hell, throw discretion to the winds.'

In 1915, Pearse gave the graveside oration at the funeral of Jeremiah O'Donovan Rossa, the old Fenian who had briefly been held in Kilmainham 50 years earlier. It was one of the supreme achievements of Irish oratory, and the concluding words have echoed down the generations: ' ... the fools, the fools, the fools! They have left us our Fenian dead, and while Ireland holds these graves,

Ireland unfree shall never be at peace.'

Pearse joined the secret Military Council of the IRB – the hardest of hard centres – in preparation for the rising. He co-wrote, with James Connolly, the Proclamation of the Republic, which he read under the portico of the GPO on Easter Monday 1916. He was chairman of the Provisional Government of the Republic, as declared.

Unlike Connolly, Pearse was not a fighting man and his military contribution to the rising was minimal, but he was the face of the rebellion and its voice. It was he, as head of the government so declared, who offered the formal surrender to the British on the Saturday.

Of course, he was court-martialled and the result was predictable. The proceedings were little better than a drumhead court martial. Pearse was returned to Kilmainham, there to walk to his death in the stonebreakers' yard on the morning of 3 May, a Sunday, one of the first three to be executed that day. He died well, a point acknowledged by the British officer in command of the firing squad.

Tom Clarke

Tom Clarke.

Thomas J. Clarke was the oldest of those executed and the most unrepentant Fenian of the lot. He was a veteran of the dynamite campaign in England in the 1880s, for which he had served 15 years in various British prisons, in conditions that left him permanently physically weakened. As a young man he had been in the United Sates, where he had come into contact with the IRB, and he enthusiastically embraced their radical policy of direct action.

He was eventually released by the British, returned briefly to the United States and married the niece of one of his close Fenian friends. Like Pearse, he became close to Devoy – without whom nothing much moved in Irish-American republican circles – and actually took out United States' citizenship.

Still, Ireland called. In 1907 he came back to Dublin, where he opened a couple of tobacconists' shops, the principal one in Parnell Street. He found the Irish Fenian organisation in a bad way, seemingly a remnant of a time long gone and just the sentimental memory-bank of withered old men.

Seán Mac Diarmada.

He took it in hand. He became a father-figure to a new generation of budding republicans, none more important than Seán Mac Diarmada, who proved to be an organiser of formidable ability. Gradually, he and Clarke rebuilt the structures of the Fenian Brotherhood. They were out-and-out militarists and intriguers, preferring conspiratorial secrecy to open declarations. With their structures duly renewed, Clarke was elected to the supreme council of the IRB.

He was also a propagandist of talent. He organised the first pilgrimage of republicans to the grave of Theobald Wolfe Tone at Bodenstown, County Kildare, a tradition honoured to this day. This was in protest against the visit of King George V to Ireland. When the radical republicans ran a shipment of arms into the little fishing port of Howth, at the northern end of Dublin Bay, Clarke was involved as well.

Tom Clarke's cell door at Kilmainham.

He was revered, a living link with the irreconcilable republican past.

Clarke was a member of the Military Council that planned and executed the rising of 1916. He was the first signatory of the Proclamation of the Republic. When the rising ended, the surrender was, by a terrible irony, delivered by Pearse to Brigadier-General Lowe of the British Army in the doorway of Tom Clarke's tobacconists in Parnell Street.

Clarke met his death before a firing squad, like Pearse, early in the morning on 3 May 1916. At 58, he was the oldest of those executed by the British. He had spent more than a quarter of his life in English prisons, admittedly for actions of which many radical republicans on both sides of the Atlantic disapproved. That was all forgotten now. In the stonebreakers' yard that Sunday morning, Tom Clarke entered the Irish republican Pantheon.

Tom Clarke's death certificate.

MEDICAL CERTIFICATE of the CAUSE of DEATH.

Countess Markievicz
escaped execution.

Leaders of the 1916
Rising, including most
of the 16 executed by
the British.

The executions occurred
on the following
days: 3 May – Pádraig
Pearse, Tom Clarke,
Thomas MacDonagh; 4
May – Joseph Plunkett,
Edward Daly, William
Pearse, Michael
O'Hanrahan; 5 May
– John MacBride; 6
May – Éamonn Ceannt,
Michael Mallin, Con
Colbert, Seán Heuston;
9 May – Thomas
Kent; 12 May – Seán
MacDermott, James
Connolly; 3 August –
Roger Casement.

Thomas MacDonagh

The third man shot that Sunday morning was Thomas MacDonagh. He was, along with Pearse, the most culturally significant of the 1916 leaders. He was born in County Tipperary in 1878 and became a teacher. He taught in a number of schools and was a founder member of the Association of Secondary Teachers. Like so many of his generation he was drawn to the Gaelic Revival movement.

He became friendly with Pádraig Pearse and eventually joined the teaching staff at St Enda's. Having completed his Master's degree at University College Dublin, he joined the staff there as a lecturer in English literature. He was co-editor of the *Irish Review* (the other co-editor was Joseph Plunkett, another man executed in 1916) and was involved in a number of other cultural and intellectual exercises.

It was a classic formation. MacDonagh was a founder member of the Irish Volunteers, for whom he became director of training. He was heavily involved in the Howth gun-running and in the organisation of the funeral of Jeremiah O'Donovan Rossa, over whose grave Pearse spoke so memorably.

Like Pearse and Connolly, he published widely, but more literary work than all the others. Principally a literary man, his main output

comprised poetry and drama. But he was scholarly too: his book *Literature in Ireland* was also published, albeit posthumously.

He became closely involved with plans for the rising of 1916. He had been a member of the IRB since the autumn of 1915 and, late in the day – just before the rising took place – he found himself a member of the ultra-secret Military Council. Moreover, he was awarded a battalion command, being placed in charge of the small garrison at Jacob's biscuit factory on the edge of the south inner city.

Jacob's biscuit factory.

Of all the 1916 garrisons, MacDonagh's saw the least action. It was an enormous industrial building, as big as any mill. It was impregnable to anything other than artillery, and the British were never going to waste precious artillery on such a strategically insignificant location. So MacDonagh and his men had a quiet week of it, as these things go.

There were tragedies nearby, none the less. Francis Sheehy-Skeffington was a pacifist, a feminist and a vegetarian given to wearing homespun tweeds in the Shavian manner. He was a good man if ever there was one, but was widely regarded as something of a holy fool. He had spent part of the Tuesday of the rising trying to restrain shop looters and was due to address a public meeting that evening. First, he decided to go to his house before returning to town. His home was not far from the Jacob's garrison. Likewise, it wasn't far from Portobello Barracks, wherein a mad British officer called Bowen-Colthurst seemed to be possessed by demons.

Francis Sheehy-Skeffington was executed in Dublin by British army officer Captain Bowen-Colthurst, on Easter Monday 1916.

The officer arrested Sheehy-Skeffington, the most harmless man in the city, and had him shot the following morning. MacDonagh may have been impregnable in Jacob's but he was impotent to stop this tragedy. Nothing much else happened, but MacDonagh, for no better reason than the command he had held, also found himself in the stonebreakers' yard.

Joseph Plunkett

Joseph Mary Plunkett.

By Irish standards, the Plunketts were well-to-do, if not downright rich. The family had originally made its money in building, although they could claim a more ancient lineage that lifted them above trade: they were a cadet branch of one of the ancient Hiberno-Norman families of the Pale, which produced such luminaries as St Oliver Plunkett and the Barons Dunsany. Many of the burgeoning Victorian middle-class suburbs on the south side of Dublin had been developed by Joseph's grandfather. So much so that Joseph's father, George Noble Plunkett, born in 1851, was able to live the life of a scholarly gentleman of independent means.

George was an enthusiast for the preservation of the Irish language, a senior figure in the Irish National Literary Society and a magazine proprietor and editor. Along the way, he became a papal count for donating money to Catholic causes, and was known ever after as George Noble, Count Plunkett. Later, he became director of the National Museum, a vice-president of the Royal Irish Academy and president of the Royal Society of Antiquaries of Ireland. All in all, he was a cultural ornament, and a most improbable father of a martyred republican revolutionary.

Joseph Mary Plunkett was born in 1887 and was educated privately at elite Jesuit schools, at Belvedere College in Dublin and Stonyhurst College in Lancashire. He was a delicate youth, having contracted the dreaded tuberculosis. He spent some time in dry Mediterranean countries in the hope of arresting the advance of the disease, this being a standard practice for those that could afford it. At Stonyhurst, his involvement with the Officer Training Corps gave him a rudimentary insight into

George Noble Plunkett KCHS (3 December 1851–12 March 1948), father of Joseph, was an Irish nationalist politician, museum director and biographer. He was MP for Roscommon North from 1917 to 1922.

military tactics which he later placed at the service of the IRB.

Back in Ireland, he joined the Gaelic League and made the classic transition towards militant republicanism. He and Thomas MacDonagh became very close friends; they had common cultural and literary interests.

He joined the IRB in 1915, becoming their principal military strategist. He went to Germany to solicit arms, where his efforts resulted in a shipment that was almost landed in County Kerry on the weekend before the rising. It was largely his plan of scattered garrisons that was carried into effect once the rising began. He himself, although now desperately ill with TB, fought as best he could with the GPO garrison.

As a signatory of the Proclamation of the Republic, Plunkett was a marked man. He was executed in the stonebreakers' yard on Monday 4 May, having married his fiancée Grace Gifford in the prison chapel at Kilmainham the night before. A book of his poetry was published posthumously.

Joseph Mary Plunkett operated the radio from the GPO training centre during the fighting.

His father, the papal count, made very old bones, living to be 97 and dying as one of the distinguished ornaments of the newly independent Irish state. Both Count and Countess Plunkett were imprisoned in Kilmainham for a time after the Rising.

During the Civil War, Grace Plunkett was arrested with many others in February 1923 and interned at Kilmainham Gaol for three months. She painted pictures on the walls of her cell, including one of the Virgin and Child. She was released in May 1923.

Grace Evelyn Gifford Plunkett (4 March 1888–13 December 1955) was active in the Republican movement. She was an artist and cartoonist, who studied under Sir William Orpen.

Edward 'Ned' Daly

Ned Daly was commander of the garrison established at the Four Courts on Easter Monday morning. His command was the only garrison, apart from that at the GPO, that lay within the cordon thrown around the city centre by the British on Tuesday morning. Even then, it was quickly cut off from the GPO when the British took control of Capel Street.

Edward Daly was the youngest commandant of the 1916 Rising.

On the Monday, the Four Courts command had made its mark. Just as the rising was getting under way, a shipment of ammunition for the British army was unloading at the North Wall. It was met by an escort from the 5th and 12th Lancers, who brought it along the quays to Marlborough (now McKee) Barracks near the Phoenix Park. This took them past the end of Sackville Street just as the Volunteers were occupying the GPO 200 metres away.

Ruins of the Linenhall Barracks, headquarters of the then British Army Pay Department, which w destroyed by members of the Four Courts garris

A few minutes later, they came upon a makeshift barrier thrown up by Daly's men at the point where Church Street met the Liffey quay. For the inexperienced Volunteers, the mounted lancers were a formidable and frightening sight. As much from terror as from any other consideration, they fired at the cavalrymen. The effect was startling. Completely taken by surprise, the lancers turned into a side street, only to come under fire from other corners of the garrison adjacent. Two of their number died in the eventual confusion.

The Four Courts saw little further action until the Friday, although they did attack the nearby Linenhall Barracks, now occupied by a few retired soldiers. They set it alight, creating a blaze that was visible all over central

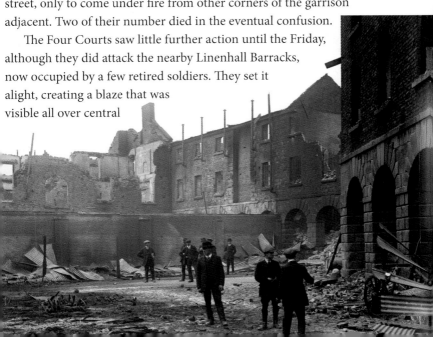

Dublin. However, the proximity of the British cordon – running along Brunswick Street just to its rear – made the Four Courts' position increasingly untenable.

As the British deployed men along the cordon, they found themselves under sniper fire from unseen enemies in civilian clothes. These were some of Daly's men. As the cordon tightened along North King Street, some of the most vicious house-to-house fighting of the entire week took place. It was Saturday morning before the last of the Four Courts' garrison were flushed from their outlying position.

Devastation in Dublin. Photo by T. W. Murphy.

In all, this battle at North King Street lasted 16 hours and cost at least 14 lives. It had brought the most concentrated and continuous fighting of the entire rising.

Ned Daly was a Fenian through and through. From Limerick, his father and uncle were leading members of the IRB. His sister Kathleen was married to Tom Clarke. After the surrender, he was held in Richmond Barracks and Kilmainham, court-martialled and sentenced to death. Of the garrison commanders executed, at 25 he was the youngest. He was shot at dawn on 4 May.

The British soldiers held as prisoners were impressed with their treatment at the Four Courts, finding Ned Daly's men both courteous and honourable.

Michael O'Hanrahan

O'Hanrahan had been a senior colleague of MacDonagh's at Jacob's factory. He was third in command after MacDonagh himself and John MacBride. He was unlucky. His brother, likewise posted to Jacob's, was also sentenced to death but his sentence was commuted. Michael's execution demonstrated the random element in the British reprisals. Not only was O'Hanrahan not a garrison commander, he had been posted to the command that saw the least action all week and which had inflicted minimal casualties on the British.

Michael O'Hanrahan.

O'Hanrahan was from New Ross, County Wexford. His family had strong Fenian connections and New Ross itself had warm and proud memories of the 1798 Rebellion: one of the key battles of that conflict was fought in the town, and was the first turning of the tide against the rebels. None the less, they were remembered with pride. Thus, O'Hanrahan came not just from a family tradition but from a community in which hostility to British rule was deeply ingrained. His father may have taken part in the Fenian rising of 1867.

As with so many other leading men of 1916, he had the classic formation of Gaelic League, Sinn Féin and the Irish Volunteers. He was a founder member of the Volunteers and was appointed quartermaster-general of the 2nd battalion. In Jacob's, his most significant intervention came at the surrender on the Saturday. The garrison was divided on the issue, some wishing to tough it out and go down with all guns blazing. It was an understandable position to take after the days of inaction.

O'Hanrahan was one of the voices recommending the acceptance of Pearse's surrender order. He reasoned that to hold out might be heroic but it would invite an artillery assault – for nothing less would shift them from such a formidable building – and would inevitably entail civilian casualties in the surrounding area, which was densely populated.

His execution displayed the chaotic thinking of the British in the aftermath of the rising. General Maxwell's orders were that death sentences should only be passed on 'ringleaders', without any definition of that term. O'Hanrahan's sentence of death was justified on grounds that were much vaguer than that. It was stated that he had been active in the Irish Volunteers and had been arrested while bearing arms. If those criteria had been consistently applied, the British would have had to execute many more than the 16 who paid the supreme penalty.

It was a tragic muddle. Michael O'Hanrahan certainly inflicted – or caused to be inflicted – less damage on the British than many who escaped the firing squad. His position at Jacob's

Cathal Brugha, who later became the first President of Dáil Éireann before being killed in the 1922 Civil War.

alone accounted for that. Moreover, others who held second-in-command positions – let alone third-in-command – were not shot: Cathal Brugha, second-in-command to Éamonn Ceannt at the South Dublin Union, was a notable case in point.

Michael O'Hanrahan is remembered in Wexford. The railway station in the town is named for him, as is the bridge across the River Barrow at New Ross.

O'Hanrahan under British army escort.

Willie Pearse.

Willie Pearse

If Michael O'Hanrahan was unlucky, what word can be deployed to explain the execution of Willie Pearse? It is hard to escape the conclusion that he was shot for nothing more than being Pádraig's brother.

Willie was younger than Pádraig by two years. He was very close to his elder brother, whom he revered. He was not academically gifted but he showed an early talent for academic sculpting, thus surpassing his father who had been a mere monumental sculptor. He studied in Dublin at the Metropolitan School of Art, where one of his teachers was Oliver Shepherd, whose statue of Cúchulain stands in the GPO to commemorate the rising. He later continued his art studies in London – at South Kensington – and in Paris.

When he returned to Dublin, he involved himself in Irish cultural bodies, including the Gaelic League, and taught Irish language classes. In all this, he was very much in his brother's shadow, although content to be so.

He showed his own work at various exhibitions in Dublin, including the Irish International Exhibition of 1907. He carried on his father's business – his father had died in 1900 – executing church commissions until the family firm closed in 1910. He was also a talented actor, appearing at the Abbey Theatre among other venues.

Like Pádraig, he was drawn to nationalist causes and was, according to some accounts, on the

Memorial plaque erected to Pádraig Pearse and William Pearse at Pearse & Sons stone masonry shop in Dublin city centre.

Pearse Museum,
St Enda's Park,
Rathfarnham.

committee that organised the centenary celebrations for the 1798 Rebellion. He was commissioned to carve the memorial to Father John Murphy that stands in Wexford town. With Pádraig, he joined the Irish Volunteers. He also taught at St Enda's, where he was effectively his brother's vice-principal, and where he formed a friendship with Thomas MacDonagh. Between them, they ensured that the school had a generous humanities curriculum.

Willie Pearse played no role of any significance in the planning of the 1916 Rising, and was not high in the counsels of those that did. He did, however, join Pádraig in the GPO garrison, where he acted as a sort of aide-de-camp without exercising any commanding role. Whenever Pádraig moved to encourage troops in exposed positions, such as on the roof of the GPO, he was invariably accompanied by Willie, heroically loyal. That was about the extent of the younger brother's rebellious ways.

He was none the less court-martialled and sentenced to death, despite meeting none of the criteria for such a sentence. It was the most flagrantly capricious example of the military response to the events of Easter Week. His execution, at dawn on 4 May, was little more than an act of judicial murder.

Along with those of the others who were shot on 4 May, here were the first warning bells for the politicians in London. It was clear that Asquith's instructions, although sloppily drafted, were being deliberately misinterpreted by Maxwell. It was to take another week, and more executions, before Asquith took the matter properly in hand and visited Dublin himself, at which point the executions stopped.

Asquith leaves Richmond Barracks on Saturday 13 May 1916, after having conversations with some of the rebel prisoners.

John MacBride

Major John MacBride, as he was generally known, was second-in-command at Jacob's. He had had the misfortune to offend W. B. Yeats, by succeeding where Yeats had failed and wooing and wedding Maud Gonne, the great love of Yeats's life. For this, naturally, Yeats never forgave him: in his great poem about the rising, 'Easter 1916', MacBride is described as 'a drunken, vainglorious lout'. It is generally a bad idea to get on the wrong side of poets.

Major John MacBride.

MacBride was born in Westport, County Mayo, to a family of small farmers and shopkeepers. He was attracted, as a young man, to the Fenians. He found them, however, at their lowest ebb, lacking energy and ambition. He was soon disillusioned, but he never completely severed his links. In the 1890s, he emigrated to South Africa, where he found employment with the Rand Mining Corporation and raised an Irish Brigade to fight for the Boers against the British in the Second Boer War (1899–1902).

He emerged from the Boer War a major and returned to Ireland, where he stood without success for a parliamentary seat in his native county. He met Maud Gonne through their mutual friend, Arthur Griffith, although Griffith counselled both of them not to get married. He was right. The marriage did not last: within two years it was over, although it had lasted long enough to produce a son, the remarkable Seán MacBride. The break-up was a bitter business, with accusations and counter-accusations that caused a public scandal.

One reason for the failure of the marriage was MacBride's well-known problem with alcohol. This didn't prevent him securing a permanent job as a water bailiff with the

Maud Gonne.

Dublin Corporation. He maintained his contacts with the IRB – he was a member of the Supreme Council – but was not part of the Military Council that planned the rising in secret. Indeed, he seems to have found himself involved on Easter Monday as much by accident as design. He turned up in smart civilian clothes as MacDonagh's men were mustering on St Stephen's Green, prior to occupying Jacob's factory. His military experience in the Boer War was enough to secure him his position.

When the surrender order came to Jacob's, it caused confusion and dispute – some doubting its authenticity. MacBride supported Michael O'Hanrahan's view that further resistance was futile. He was arrested, court-martialled and sentenced to death. The sentence was carried out on the morning of 5 May. Again, his execution demonstrated the random and inconsistent nature of the sentences handed down. It was difficult to see why he was made to pay the supreme penalty. He was not a significant figure either in revolutionary circles or in the rising itself and it is hard not to conclude

Major John MacBride is arrested, depicted on the front page of the *Daily Sketch*, 8 May 1916.

that residual prejudice for his part in the Boer War prejudiced the military tribunal.

A monument to Major John MacBride in Westport, County Mayo.

Con Colbert

Con Colbert (1888–1916) was another relatively minor figure to be shot in the stonebreakers' yard in Kilmainham. His death was yet further evidence of the random nature of the death sentences handed down by the military tribunal in the fervid atmosphere following the rising, before the politicians got a grip on things and took control of events back from the army.

Con Colbert.

Colbert was from County Limerick. His family had strong Fenian sympathies, with which he quickly associated himself. He too had a classic republican formation: he was an Irish language enthusiast, fluent from an early age, and a member of the Gaelic League. He also joined Na Fianna Éireann, a republican youth movement founded by Bulmer Hobson and Constance Markievicz and loosely modelled on the Boy Scouts. His abilities were quickly spotted and eventually he became its chief national instructor.

Na Fianna was also a recruiting platform for the IRB and Colbert was duly inducted. He was an active instructor for Na Fianna, having acquired a high level of proficiency in military drill. In time, this brought him to the attention of Pádraig Pearse, who engaged him as a drill instructor at his school, St Enda's, a position for which Colbert declined any remuneration. For Pearse, it was not simply that Colbert could impart his knowledge of drill and associated military skills, but that he could do so through the medium of the Irish language.

Bulmer Hobson.

Con Colbert was a rigorist, deeply religious and – in common with so many advanced nationalists of his generation – hostile to alcohol, which he blamed for many republican and radical failures in the past.

In the Easter Rising, he was assigned to the 4th battalion under Éamonn Ceannt and Cathal Brugha, whose headquarters were at the South Dublin

Jameson's Distillery,
Marrowbone Lane.

Union. He was placed in command of a small group of Volunteers who took up their position at a brewery in Ardee Street in the Liberties, with the intention of engaging British Army reinforcements on their way from Richmond Barracks in Inchicore to positions in the city centre.

Apart from some minor engagements, the outpost saw little action there. Colbert moved his men instead to Jameson's Distillery in Marrowbone Lane, from which they provided an effective sniping fire directed at the British. This action took some of the pressure off the principal battalion position at the South Dublin Union, where the fighting was ferocious.

As with the 2nd battalion at Jacob's, the news of the general surrender on the Saturday was at first received with scepticism and incredulity by Colbert and his men. They were isolated, and had lost contact with the rest of the rising, including their own battalion headquarters at the SDU.

Colbert was an effective and disciplined operator, but his role in the rising was still a minor one. Indeed, his skills might have merited a more substantial command. None the less, he was sentenced to death, yet another figure of whom it could be said that his actions scarcely merited such a harsh judgment. He was shot on 8 May. The railway station in Limerick city is named for him.

The South Dublin Union in the 1950s.

Éamonn Ceannt

Ceannt was a signatory of the Proclamation of the Republic, so his death sentence was predictable. All seven signatories were executed, so that at least the military tribunal was consistent in that if in little else.

Éamonn Ceannt.

He was born Edward Kent in County Galway, the son of an Irish-speaking RIC man who was transferred to County Louth. When Kent senior retired, he moved his family to Dublin, where his son completed his education. He was intelligent and a good linguist: he became fluent in Irish, helped by his father, and quickly adopted the Irish-language form of his name. He was also proficient in French and German. Moreover, he was a good musician and an accomplished player of the uilleann pipes: he was a co-founder of the Dublin Pipers' Club and played for Pope Pius X while on a visit to Rome.

From an early age, Ceannt was drawn to advanced nationalist causes. As a youth, he was inspired by the centenary celebrations for the 1798 Rebellion. He joined Sinn Féin and was elected to its national council. He worked for the Dublin Corporation in the city treasurer's office and wrote frequently for nationalist periodicals and journals in both Irish and English. He was intellectually curious and well read, more so than many advanced nationalists who often had a narrower focus. He was politically to the left of many in Sinn Féin; he supported the locked-out workers in the great Dublin trade dispute of 1913, unlike Arthur Griffith, who saw trade union activity as detrimental to the national economy.

Ceannt had a puritan streak – he was a non-smoking teetotaller – but was also a dedicated and disciplined person. In 1911, he was inducted into the IRB and eventually became a member of its supreme council. He was a founder member of the Irish Volunteers in 1913, took part in the Howth gun-running in July 1914 and was a prominent advocate of an insurrection while Britain was engaged in the First World War.

He was director of communications for the Irish Volunteers. Even more significant was his position in the IRB; he was part of the secret Military Council that planned and executed the Easter Rising, despite the formal Fenian leadership being kept in the dark. This meant that Ceannt was sufficiently trusted to stand at the very heart of conspiratorial politics.

Éamonn Ceannt holding a set of uilleann pipes.

During the rising, he held the rank of commandant and was at the head of the 4th battalion, whose headquarters were at the South Dublin Union. This commanded one of the principal routes into the city centre from the west. It was also supposed to cover British troops arriving by train at nearby Kingsbridge (now Heuston) Station, but lack of numbers foiled that plan.

Lack of numbers did not, however, prevent the 4th battalion from conducting some of the fiercest fighting of the week at the South Dublin Union. In confined spaces, and often close to terrified inmates, they held their positions against greater

British numbers until the general surrender order reached them. Éamonn Ceannt was shot in the stonebreakers' yard on 8 May.

Thomas MacDonagh telling Éamonn Ceannt to give the message to surrender.

Seán Heuston

Seán Heuston.

Seán Heuston was a Dubliner, a clerk on the Great Southern and Western Railway, whose main Dublin terminus, Kingsbridge Station, was renamed for him in 1966. He was a member of Na Fianna and the Irish Volunteers. Like his friend Con Colbert, he was a part-time drill instructor at St Enda's, Pádraig Pearse's school at Rathfarnham, Dublin. At the time of the Howth gun-running in July 1914, he commanded a Fianna troop that helped unload the artillery from the *Asgard*.

On Easter Monday 1916, he was ordered by James Connolly to seize the Mendicity Institute at Usher's Island on the south quays of the Liffey. Technically, he was part of the 1st battalion under Edward Daly, which was based in the Four Courts just across the river, but the order to take the Mendicity, a poorhouse, appears to have come direct from the commandant-general of republican forces. Heuston and his men travelled along the south quays by tram before occupying the Mendicity.

The position was chosen because it was along the most obvious route for British troops to take from Kingsbridge Station to the city centre, and troops from the Curragh did indeed begin to arrive at Kingsbridge from early on Tuesday morning. In addition, the Mendicity provided cover for the larger Four Courts garrison opposite, although Edward Daly had had nothing to do with Heuston's presence there. Connolly had envisaged this outpost as no more than a temporary expedient. Accordingly, it was starved of rations and ammunition, since no one had expected it to be still functioning on the third day of the rising.

Amazingly, it was. Heuston's men were outnumbered by ten to one. None the less, they inflicted over a hundred casualties on the British before they were eventually surrounded. Had they

Seán Heuston monument in Phoenix Park, Dublin, by Lawrence Campbell, 1943.

beaten a tactical retreat the previous day, they would at a minimum have got away and might even have been able to join the main battalion position across the river in the Four Courts. However, by Wednesday they had made such a thorough nuisance of themselves that the British committed serious numbers to rooting them out. They took over rising ground at the rear of the Mendicity, leading up towards Thomas Street, which gave them a free field of fire. The final assault began at noon and lasted an hour. The British troops were from the Dublin Fusiliers, one group of whom made the decisive move. Under covering fire, they got to the front wall of the Mendicity and threw bombs through the window, creating havoc inside. Four Volunteers died.

About 15 minutes of this elapsed before Heuston hung out the white flag and the Mendicity Institute became the first rebel position to surrender. It had been, in all the circumstances, an astonishing stand. However, it effectively placed Heuston in the position of having exercised an independent command, and that put him in the way of danger. Seán Heuston was condemned to death by the military tribunal and was executed on the morning of 8 May. He was 25 years of age.

Heuston was told to hold the Mendicity for three or four hours, to delay the advance of British troops. He held it for more than two days, with 26 Volunteers.

Moira House, home of the Mendicity Institute, as it would have looked in 1752.

Michael Mallin

Michael Mallin (1874–1916) is one of the less well-remembered leaders of the rising who died in Kilmainham Gaol. This is a pity, for he was in so many respects a man of great gifts and natural bearing. He was born in the Liberties, had only a primary school education and joined the British Army as a drummer boy.

Michael Mallin.

It was not just the drums, however. He was musically talented and he gained proficiency in playing both the violin and the flute, as well as studying the elements of musical theory. He and his battalion were posted to India, where Mallin saw action on the North-West Frontier. India troubled him and he became ever more doubtful of the imperial role, finding the case for Indian independence ever more compelling.

He returned to Ireland on his discharge from the army in 1902, married and found employment as a silk weaver. A sympathy for the underdog that reflected his feelings in India drew him to the trade union movement and he became secretary of the Silk Weavers' Union, leading its members in a four-month strike in 1913. It cost him his job – he was dismissed for his part in the strike.

By then, Mallin had involved himself in left-wing and labour politics; he was a founder member of the Socialist Party of Ireland. To compensate for his loss of income, he was able to earn money by giving private music lessons and he conducted a number of bands, including the Irish Transport and General Workers' Union's Emmet Fife and Drum Band.

This brought him close to James Connolly's circle. It also led Mallin into the Irish Citizen Army, the tiny labour militia formed by Connolly to protect workers against police attacks. Connolly appointed Mallin as his chief-of-staff. Mallin's military experience was of immense value to the Citizen Army; indeed, of all the leaders of 1916, he

James Connolly founded the Irish Citizen Army, along with James Larkin and Jack White, on 23 November 1913.

and Connolly had the most practical experience from their days with the British Army.

The rising was jointly conducted by the Irish Volunteers and the Citizen Army. Mallin was placed in command of a garrison at St Stephen's Green – and it was here that his good sense appears to have abandoned him. He occupied the green itself on Easter Monday and dug himself in as if it were the Western Front. No sooner were his men entrenched than it rained hard: the night of Easter Monday brought the only bad weather of an otherwise lovely spring week.

The Shelbourne Hotel in the late 19th century.

By the Tuesday, the British had delivered troops into Dublin, some of whom were sent up to Stephen's Green. They did the obvious and occupied the Shelbourne Hotel – the tallest structure surrounding the green itself and commanding an excellent strategic position. Even better from their perspective, they got some Vickers machine guns to the upper floors. Mallin's garrison took some losses and retreated to the far side of St Stephen's Green, occupying the strategically negligible College of Surgeons, where they accomplished very little for the rest of the week and were short of rations.

Michael Mallin was court-martialled, sentenced to death and executed in Kilmainham on 8 May.

The British Army brought in machine guns, which the rebels did not have.

Seán Mac Diarmada

Seán Mac Diarmada.

Seán Mac Diarmada (MacDermott in English) was the key organiser in the revival of the IRB from the moribund position in which he found it. More than anyone else, he furnished the musculature necessary for the rising. The Fenians of 10 years earlier could not possibly have pulled off such a coup, even in promising circumstances. They were old men, and tired, and much given to reminiscing over a drink.

Mac Diarmada was born in County Leitrim in 1883. He worked for a while in Scotland and in Belfast. There, he joined a Dungannon Club, an early militant group, and this eventually led to his membership of the IRB. He was appointed a local organiser of the IRB in Ulster, where his energy and focus delivered results. This brought him into the national sphere. In 1908, he was appointed national organiser of the IRB. By a happy coincidence, Tom Clarke, the most unrepentant Fenian of them all, had returned to Ireland the previous year, and he and Mac Diarmada made a complementary pair.

Mac Diarmada travelled all over Ireland, inducting advanced nationalist young men into the IRB and allied organisations. In every county in Ireland he developed a huge network of contacts, on whose good offices he could call for advice or local information. He spearheaded the drive to infiltrate other nationalist organisations – the GAA was an obvious one – and saw to it that, as far as he could, reliable men of Fenian sympathies were placed in positions of influence in these organisations.

Seán Mac Diarmada had never heard of Italian political theorist Antonio Gramsci, who was to recommend left-wing activists to engage 'in a long march through the institutions'. None the less, that's exactly what Mac Diarmada was doing. He did not succeed simply by formally augmenting IRB numbers but by seeding cultural Fenianism through the wider nationalist mind.

Late 19th centiury Royal Avenue, Belfast.

In 1913, Mac Diarmada was elected secretary of the IRB supreme council, with Clarke as treasurer. He was closely involved in the foundation of the Irish Volunteers, ensuring that it too had a strong Fenian element. This became even more pronounced over the split with John Redmond at the start of the First World War, with the minority who retained the Irish Volunteer name containing even more radicals and irreconcilables proportionately. When the war came, Mac Diarmada served four months in prison for making anti-recruiting speeches.

Just before the rising, Tom Clarke had him inducted on to the Military Council which was planning the insurrection in secret. He was a signatory of the Proclamation of the Republic and served in the GPO during Easter Week. He was unable to do much: an attack of polio in 1911 had left him an invalid for many months and disabled thereafter, although he did act as aide-de-camp to James Connolly.

However, as a signatory of the Proclamation his death was certain. He conducted a robust defence

Michael Collins was the last president of the IRB.

The Proclamation was printed in Liberty Hall the day before the Rising. The use of different typefaces was due to a shortage of type as a result of police raids on the building. Only around 2,500 copies were printed and they were either left around to be picked up by passers-by or posted up in the nearby streets. One of only 50 copies thought to survive was sold at auction in 2015 for €420,000.

of his actions and person at the court martial, but – despite growing public unrest – he was executed in the stonebreakers' yard at Kilmainham on 12 May.

James Connolly

Connolly was the last man to die, on 12 May. He had been born in Edinburgh almost 48 years earlier, into a crushingly poor Irish immigrant community. He joined the British Army at fourteen and served seven years in Ireland. Back in Scotland, the socialist John Leslie became a seminal influence. He arranged for Connolly to go to Dublin to work for the Dublin Socialist Society.

James Connolly.

Within two years, in 1898, Connolly had founded the Irish Socialist Republican Party and a short-lived newspaper, the *Workers' Republic*. He had made a lifetime commitment to socialism back in Scotland, where he read everything on the subject that he could secure; he was hugely influenced by

Marx and Engels, but also – closer to home – by Leslie. Now he had to spread the word in the unpromising territory of Ireland.

Many advanced nationalists were suspicious of socialism and the labour movement, seeing it variously as atheistic and British, and a menace to the development of an indigenous Irish economy and society. Naturally, the huge moral influence of the Catholic Church was relentlessly deployed against it.

So Connolly had to confront the reality of nationalism, not something generally congenial to the international socialist mind. He did so none the less, for he came to realise that socialism could only prosper if anchored in the legitimacy that republican nationalism could alone deliver. It was a highly original compound, the product of a fertile and subtle intelligence.

Connolly's reputation grew to the point that he received an invitation from the Socialist Labour Party of America to make a lecture tour of the United States in 1902–3. The tour helped to relieve his chronic financial difficulties. After a brief time back in Ireland, he returned to the United States, where he worked as a union organiser for seven years.

He still maintained his contacts with the small labour movement in Dublin. That movement received an enormous shot in the arm in 1907 with the arrival of the titanic figure of James Larkin. In 1909, Larkin founded the ITGWU, drawing in semi-skilled and unskilled workers. Connolly came back to Ireland in 1910 and effectively became Larkin's second-in-command, wrote a couple of influential books, and helped Larkin during the great lockout of Dublin workers in the autumn of 1913. The workers lost; Larkin went to the United States, and Connolly became head of the ITGWU.

The quickening atmosphere in republican circles caused by British involvement in the First World War deepened Connolly's belief in the necessity for the labour struggle to harmonise with the republican cause. He committed his small labour militia to the rising and was appointed commandant-general, or military commander. On the Thursday, while checking an outpost, a sniper's bullet shattered his ankle and he was carried back into the GPO in agony.

After the surrender, he faced the court martial and was sentenced to death. He was carried by stretcher to Kilmainham where – surprisingly for a socialist – he made a

James Larkin speaking to a crowd.

final confession to a priest, was placed on a chair in the stonebreakers' yard, blindfolded but unbound, and shot. His execution aroused particular public revulsion, and he was the last of the participants in the rising to be executed at Kilmainham.

Connolly was not held in prison, but in a room (now called the Connolly Room) at the State Apartments in Dublin Castle, which had been converted to a first-aid station for troops recovering from the war.

Ghosts

There is a persistent rumour that Kilmainham Gaol is or was haunted. When I started writing this book, I mentioned what I was doing to someone who said, 'Oh, there are lots of ghost stories about Kilmainham. You should put them in. People will be really fascinated by them.'

There are no ghosts in Kilmainham and there never have been. A former senior official of the museum was often there until 11pm at night – alone. Nothing. Once, for sheer amusement, he allowed a member of the British Poltergeist Association to spend a night in the place carrying out 'tests'. Still nothing.

The nearest thing to a para-normal event in the entire history of the gaol was a cell door that would be found open in the morning even though it was known that it had been locked the night before. That is the sum total of ghosts, poltergeists and things that go bump in the night in the history of Kilmainham Gaol.

History is about stuff that happens. Fiction is about stuff that doesn't happen, or hasn't happened. *Hamlet* never happened; nor did *The Simpsons* or anything by Charles Dickens or Jeffrey Archer. Even where novelists draw on things that did happen – history – they use it not for itself but to suit the structure and contour of their fiction. Dickens's treatment of the French Revolution in *A Tale of Two Cities* is a case in point.

Hundreds of novelists have used historical events as their raw material, but the events of Dublin on 16 June 1904 are not as Joyce described them in *Ulysses*, even though some of the specifics here and there did happen. Joyce simply used these bits and pieces to serve his larger fictional purposes. There are hundreds of other examples: Salman Rushdie, Joseph Heller, Hilary Mantel and a whole stable full of popular novelists who draw on historical themes for their fiction.

Historical fiction is still fiction. It's still stuff that didn't happen, or didn't happen in the manner set out in these works of the imagination. So I'm

sorry to disappoint my friend who was so certain that there was a great archive of ghost stories in Kilmainham Gaol lying about awaiting discovery by a diligent researcher. I am that person and I am here to report that there is nothing there: nothing to see. Be good enough to move along, ladies and gentlemen: thank you very much.

At the risk of repeating myself and boring the patient reader, let me state once and for all that there are no ghosts and goblins in Kilmainham Gaol, nor have there ever been.

Unless you count that open cell door, of course.

Éamon de Valera

Éamon de Valera was the only holder of an independent command in the Easter Rising of 1916 not to be executed by the British. He commanded the 3rd battalion of the Irish Volunteers, which occupied Boland's Mills on the south-eastern edge of the city centre. Its basic purpose was to stop or delay any troop movements by train into nearby Westland Row (now Pearse) Station. This was the city terminus for the line running in from Kingstown (now Dún Laoghaire), the obvious disembarkation point for any relief troops sent from Britain.

Éamon de Valera.

The troops landed at Kingstown, but instead of travelling onwards by train they marched into town. An outpost of de Valera's command set up at Mount Street Bridge by the Grand Canal and caught the incoming troops in a hard-fought battle on the Wednesday afternoon. They inflicted the heaviest losses of the week on the British by occupying the tall houses that commanded the

A captured de Valera under
escort by British soldiers.

Sinéad de Valera was a teacher and author of over 20 children's books in both Irish and English. She married Éamon de Valera in 1910.

bridge and its approach road. In all, there were only twelve Volunteers, eight of whom paid with their lives. Between them, they inflicted 230 dead or wounded on the British.

So when it came to the military tribunal in the aftermath, it looked bleak for de Valera. Not only had he run an independent command, his men had inflicted the most casualties of the week on British troops. Yet his life was spared. Why? One officer prosecuting before the tribunal, an Irishman, was asked by Maxwell who was next on the list. By now, it was 8 May and the political heat was being felt by the military. The executions were going down badly with the public. Maxwell was told that Éamon de Valera was next.

Maxwell asked if de Valera was likely to be any future trouble and the officer said he thought not. But he was tried anyway, a sentence of death was passed upon him and he was taken to Kilmainham and lodged in cell 59. Why was he not shot? It was almost certainly because he held United States citizenship (he had been born in New York City). It was one thing to shoot Irishmen who were technically British subjects. It was quite another to shoot one who had an American passport at a time when Britain and the Allies were desperate to get the United States into the First World War. The matter will never be decided: the American connection – and some vigorous lobbying by de Valera's wife, Sinéad – was one factor. Growing public unrest was another.

So de Valera was not shot. He was moved first to Mountjoy, on the far side of Dublin, and then to Dartmoor. Within a year, he was out and well on his way to being the leader of Sinn Féin and the undisputed leader of nationalist Ireland.

Of course, that did not last. De Valera took the anti-Treaty side after the split and in 1923 was once again lodged in Kilmainham, this time by a native Irish government. He found the prison 'an awful place', although he was kept separate from the other republicans and allowed to exercise alone. He spent three months there before being transferred to Arbour Hill and eventually released in July 1924.

De Valera's cell at Kilmainham.

Constance Markievicz

Thus far, this has been almost wholly a story about men. Women have only appeared incidentally, as wives, fiancées, housemaids or prostitutes. Now, as Kilmainham Gaol nears the end of its life as a prison, that changes. After the 1916 Rising, one of the iconic figures of the republican tradition was briefly incarcerated there.

Constance Georgine Markievicz, née Gore-Booth, was an improbable republican rebel, but rebel she was none the less. She was born into a family settled in Ireland since the Cromwellian plantations of the 1640s. Their seat was at Lissadell, a gloomy neo-Grecian pile in County Sligo, although the family spent time on the continent and in London during the social season. Constance 'came out' in society in 1887 when she was presented to Queen Victoria at Buckingham Palace.

Her passion was for fine art, of which her family disapproved – not suitable for 'gels' – but she eventually did get to study at the Slade School in London and later in Paris. There, she met her husband: Count Casimir Markievicz, an indigent member of the Polish-Ukrainian aristocracy. They settled in Dublin in 1902 and were soon a glittering couple in the rather desiccated, provincial social life of the city.

The Countess, as she was ever after known – even when she and Casimir had separated – embraced the causes of labour and republicanism. She supported women's suffrage, founded male and female republican youth groups, protested noisily against the visit to Ireland of King George V in 1911 – for which she was

Opposite:
Painting by Kasimir Dunin Markievicz, husband of Constance. *The Artist's Wife, Constance, Comtesse de Markievicz (1868–1927), Irish Painter and Revolutionary,* 1899.

Markievicz brandishing a gun in a coloured version of a studio photograph of 1915.

arrested – and joined Sinn Féin. She was a heroic traitor to her class.

During the great lockout of workers by the Dublin employers in 1913, the Countess established soup kitchens for impoverished families. She was elected honorary treasurer of the Irish Citizen Army on its foundation. She was a force of nature, flamboyant and theatrical, but adored by the poor to whose interests she had devoted her life and her energies.

In Easter Week 1916, she was second-in-command to Michael Mallin in the St Stephen's Green garrison, unfortunately not one of the more distinguished commands of the rising. Dressed in full uniform and under arms, she stood accused of killing an unarmed policeman in cold blood on the Monday, a charge that has been disputed.

She too faced the military tribunal once it was all over. She was sentenced to death but the sentence was commuted. At least in this detail, the politicians' instructions were crystal clear: no women were to be shot. She was, however, immured in Kilmainham

Countess Markievicz at Liberty Hall when she was released from prison in 1919.

Gaol, probably the most famous woman of the many who had seen the inside of that grim place.

Later, she was the first woman ever elected to the House of Commons, although she declined to take her seat on the Sinn Féin abstentionist principle, leaving Lady Astor to become the first woman to sit in the British parliament later on. The Countess remained, for the rest of her short life – she died at 59 in 1927 – a reliable supporter of every radical and advanced cause. She took the anti-Treaty side in the Civil War. She had been loved by the poor, and rightly so.

Constance Markievicz In the back of a prison van with a nurse after her arrest in Dublin.

The War of Independence

The Irish War of Independence was fought from January 1919 to July 1921, when a truce was agreed with the British. This led to the Anglo-Irish Treaty, signed in December 1921. The terms were for 26 of the 32 counties of Ireland to become a self-governing dominion within the British Empire, which fell short of the full republican demand for outright, untrammelled independence. This split the nationalist movement and in turn precipitated the Civil War of 1922–23.

Michael Collins as a young recruit.

The Easter Rising of 1916 had been tripped off by a secret cabal within the Irish Volunteers, a nationalist militia. The Volunteers mutated in the next few years into the Irish Republican Army (IRA), which was the force that conducted the War of Independence. The climactic day of the war came in Dublin on Bloody Sunday, 21 November 1920. Early that morning, members of Michael Collins's 'Squad' killed

14 members of the so-called 'Cairo Gang', a network of suspected British spies; at least eight of the gang were indeed spies. Many of them were shot while still in their beds.

That afternoon, in a reprisal attack by British Auxiliaries at Croke Park, the headquarters of the GAA, thirteen men, including one player, were killed during a football match between Dublin and Tipperary. The principal stand in Croke Park was subsequently named in honour of the dead Tipperary goalkeeper, Michael Hogan.

Michael Hogan. The British, led by the Auxiliaries, a paramilitary unit of the RIC, and supported by the Black and Tans, raided Croke Park and started firing five minutes after the match began.

Not all the Squad's targets died. Some fought back and some escaped. At 22 Lower Mount Street, one of the Squad, Frank Teeling, was wounded and subsequently arrested while trying to retreat. He was tried by court martial, sentenced to death and lodged in Kilmainham. Two of his fellow IRA prisoners in Kilmainham were Ernie O'Malley – later to gain acclaim as a writer of real talent – and Simon Donnelly.

On 14 February 1921, all three escaped from the prison. There is little doubt that their escapes were an inside job. The effect on IRA morale was tremendous, for it was a classic case of derring-do. The commander of British troops in Ireland, General Nevil Macready, declared that 'we have had a real disaster. The man Teeling and two other important men escaped last night from Kilmainham Prison and got clear away. It is about the worst blow I have had for a very long time, and I am naturally furious.'

These escapes, astonishingly, were facilitated, not by prison warders – for there were none in Kilmainham now that it was a purely military facility – but by two members of the 2nd battalion, Welsh Regiment,

Frank Teeling.

Private Ernest Roper and Private James Holland. The IRA were not squeamish, least of all Collins and his ruthless Squad, but they were assertive. The escapes were seen in nationalist Ireland as part of a benign drama, in which Irish people were no longer passive, but asserting in uncompromising terms their desire to be shot of Britain.

It was one of the very few escapes in the long history of Kilmainham. It had proved a near impregnable fortress, which could only be breached by an inside job, as with Teeling, O'Malley and Donnelly. How the crowds cheered.

Simon Donnelly at the gate through which the escapees left Kilmainham Gaol.

General Nevil Macready, in 1915.

The Civil War

The rising had changed everything. Public life in nationalist Ireland was transformed. Although Sinn Féin had had nothing to do with it, it became the political beneficiary as everyone – including the British – dubbed the rising the Sinn Féin rebellion. And so Sinn Féin changed itself from a marginal movement to a mainstream political party, eclipsing the old Parliamentary party under Redmond in the process. Éamon de Valera was its leader and he would dominate Irish political life for the first half of the century.

As leader of Fianna Fáil, Éamon de Valera became the first Taoiseach in 1937.

The island was partitioned, to the satisfaction of the Ulster unionists but to the consternation of northern nationalists, now trapped in a statelet set up for the exclusive convenience of their tribal enemy. A treaty was agreed between Sinn Féin and the British which created the Irish Free State in the rest of the island. However, Sinn Féin split over the terms and there was a short, nasty civil war from June 1922 to April 1923.

It claimed the lives of more than 1,000 people, including Arthur Griffith and Michael Collins. It also found Éamon de Valera on the anti-Treaty side. The new Free State government was uncompromising. One of its measures was to turn Kilmainham Gaol into a military prison. The number of anti-Treaty prisoners was growing all the time, as the Free State forces swept to victory, so they

On 14 April 1922 the Four Courts complex was occupied by IRA forces opposed to the Anglo-Irish Treaty, led by Rory O'Connor. The new National Army attacked the building, which was destroyed in the process.

had to be accommodated somewhere, and a near-empty existing prison offered an obvious solution.

Things got so desperate for the anti-Treaty side that prisoners in jails all over Ireland went on hunger strike, beginning on 13 October 1922. There were about 12,000 prisoners in all, of whom it was claimed that about 8,000 were refusing food. This was a mistake and recognised as such at the time. It would have made more sense to have some tough, headline strikers who might – like Terence MacSwiney – actually have run the course.

Frank Aiken, de Valera's right-hand man, may have been harbouring his own doubts when he made a rather desperate plea to the hunger strikers to stick it out to the very end, with no one breaking ranks. He told the officer commanding republican prisoners in Kilmainham: 'Under no circumstances, even should a comrade die, are you to call off the hunger strike – of course you have no power to order any man off. I believe your fight will do more for the cause than a thousand years war.' By mid-November, the hunger strikes were over. Two men had died.

Éamon de Valera himself was one of the last ever prisoners to be held in Kilmainham. The prison was coming to the end of its life. There had been too much history, too much tragedy and too much republican martyrdom for it to continue as an ordinary prison facility.

There was a tragic coda. The growing bitterness of the Civil War and the absolute determination of the new Dublin government to fight it to a successful finish led to draconian legislation, which decreed death for anyone caught in possession of a lethal weapon. In November, four republicans were executed in Kilmainham, the first of a series of such killings. It worked in the short term: the armed resistance to the new state collapsed a few months later. It left a bitter legacy for years.

Government troops escorting a prisoner in 1923 in Ballyseedy.

A Prison for Women

The government of the Irish Free State – the pro-Treaty section of Sinn Féin – asserted itself in the face of the Civil War insurgency. The conflict lasted less than a year and resulted in a decisive defeat for diehard republicanism. In the meantime, Michael Collins was the strongman of the new regime.

He re-opened Kilmainham as a military prison under the direction of Seán Ó Muirthile, one of his most trusted associates. By September 1922, after Collins's death, there were in all about 5,000 prisoners held in various prisons around Ireland.

Demand for space was such that there were exploratory talks with the British about the possibility of sending republican prisoners to the Seychelles or to St Helena! In the end, the Curragh Camp became available. The final prisoner count rose to 12,000.

The Curragh Camp was a British Army base until 1922, when it was handed over to the Irish Free State. It is now the main training centre for the Irish Army.

What was distinctive about Kilmainham during the Civil War was the number of women prisoners that it held. In all, there were more than 300 women in the gaol. This reflected the growing number and influence of women in the wider nationalist and republican movement in the wake of 1916, and also of the marked tendency of women to take the anti-Treaty side in the split. This was remarked upon contemporaneously, with no shortage of misogynistic jokes.

A field study at the gaol in 2013 attempted to recover as much of this female prisoner experience as possible. The study used the ingenious technique of interrogating the thousands of graffiti left on the prison walls by female hands. Thus, for example, we know who these women were from occasional and incomplete prison lists but also by the simple means of women inscribing their names, where they were from and the reasons for their incarceration. Some of these graffiti give the details of the women's arrests, the name of the arresting officer, and where the arrest took place.

Grace Gifford was with the ICA's St Stephen's Green contingent with Countess Markievicz. She supervised provisions in the College of Surgeons, commandeering food from shops and bread vans. She was arrested at the surrender and jailed in Kilmainham Gaol.

Other graffiti were more elaborate and sophisticated. Slogans and ballad lyrics that had once been directed at the British were now turned against the new Free State authorities. Unsurprisingly, other radical feminist issues of the day also featured, so that suffragette concerns, for example, found expression on the walls of the gaol.

Overall, the civil war experience for women at Kilmainham was an exercise in consciousness raising, bringing into focus the growing place of women in the Irish public sphere. One cell was nicknamed 'the republican sisterhood'. Women's autograph books are now held in the museum, bearing unambiguous testimony to the intersection of republican and feminist concerns. The Irish language was also a sure and certain marker of political and cultural allegiance; it is widely distributed in the autograph books. There has always been a high correlation between radical republicanism and proficiency in Irish.

In 1923, an Easter Rising commemoration ceremony, led by women who had been either related to or married to the executed leaders, took place in the gaol. As a result of the remarkable field research, it has

Graffiti over a cell doorway.

proved possible to generate the names and places of origin of most of these women detainees. As the prison approached the end of its purposed existence, we have recovered real lives that, in a previous age, would have disappeared without trace.

Free State soldiers take a break from fighting on the street in Dublin during the Civil War.

The Prison Closes

Kilmainham Gaol had seen its last prisoner by 1924 when Éamon de Valera and some others were transferred to Arbour Hill, a short distance away across the river. The government took the view that Kilmainham could no longer operate as a conventional prison. Quite apart from any problems arising from the building's age and condition, there was the weight of its history.

Robert Erskine Childers before heading to the Boer War in South Africa.

Too much of the Irish struggle for independence had either touched the prison on Gallows Hill or been immediately contained within its walls. Of the latter, the executions of 14 of the 16 men of 1916 in the stonebreakers' yard were foremost.

The four executions of republican prisoners in November 1922 – the start of a ruthless campaign of reprisals – had cast a kind of malignant spell on the place. It is easy to understand how, to contemporaries whose memories were vivid and recent, the place seemed cursed. So they just closed it, locked it up and walked away.

From time to time during the 1920s, proposals were floated with a view to re-opening Kilmainham as a prison. None of them succeeded, probably because no one in authority had the stomach – or, equally likely, the budget – for such an endeavour. All such plans were finally scotched in 1929, leaving the prison just glowering there, a sullen lump of stone, idle and crumbling. In 1932, however, it was proposed as a hostelry for those attending the Eucharistic Congress, another idea that didn't catch on.

So nothing was done. Even the change of government in 1932, which brought de Valera and his republican supporters to power, in an astonishing example of peaceful regime change considering the enmities of the Civil War only a decade earlier, made no difference. De Valera's own opinion of the place was, naturally, completely negative, so it might be imagined that he harboured no affection for the place of his incarceration.

Still, Kilmainham Gaol, for good and ill, had played a notable part in the freedom narrative. So it is strange that so little was done, although – to be fair – the state was poor and such public funds as were available were being deployed in slum clearance and the building of new working-class suburbs in the north-west and south-west of Dublin. Thus, a native government, strapped for funds, was still able to defeat a problem to which British administrations had provided no solutions. Not enough cash was left over to restore sites of memory, especially when much of that memory was sinister.

The empty prison, which had sat astride the old inner suburbs of Kilmainham and Inchicore, now found itself girdled with huge, new public housing areas, of which Ballyfermot was the nearest. Not far away, just beyond the Grand Canal, were Drimnagh and Crumlin. The whole social contour of south-west Dublin was being transformed and there, at its heart, stood Kilmainham Gaol, mouldering away in glum decay.

Kilmainham Gaol from Emmet Road.

Neglect and Restoration

The early governments of independent Ireland neglected Kilmainham Gaol, doing nothing at all to maintain the fabric of the place.

A bizarre proposal emerged in the late 1920s. The great German civil engineering enterprise of Siemens-Schuckert were building the hydro-electric scheme on the lower River Shannon just above Limerick and requested the use of Kilmainham Gaol as a holding yard for heavy goods and other kit. Why Kilmainham? Well, it was only up the road from Kingsbridge (now Heuston) railway station, from which stuff held at Kilmainham could be sent south by rail to Limerick.

The Germans' proposal would have necessitated the destruction of the west wing of the old prison, the location of the stonebreakers' yard, where the 14 martyrs of 1916 had been shot. Incredible as it seems at this remove, the authorities had no objection. In the event, however, there was no destruction.

From the 1930s on, the National Graves Association (NGA), a republican ginger group dedicated to commemorating and maintaining

HELP

THE KILMAINHAM JAIL RESTORATION SOCIETY

WHO ARE RESTORING THE JAIL BY VOLUNTARY EFFORT AS A NATIONAL MONUMENT TO THE DEAD WHO DIED FOR IRELAND.

IT WILL HOUSE A HISTORICAL MUSEUM. IF YOU LIVE IN DUBLIN COME AND WORK WITH US !

IF YOU LIVE TOO FAR AWAY SEND US WHAT HELP YOU CAN !

IF YOU HAVE ANY LETTERS, DOCUMENTS OR OBJECTS RELATING TO THE STRUGGLE FOR INDEPENDENCE, REMEMBER THE KILMAINHAM MUSEUM.

Write to us at

KILMAINHAM JAIL, DUBLIN

THE JAIL IS OPEN TO VISITORS ON SUNDAYS 3 to 5 P.M.

the graves of Ireland's patriot dead, took up the cause of Kilmainham Gaol. They were supremely conscious of it as a site of memory, and in particular of republican memory. They lobbied the government, unsuccessfully. Nothing happened until after the Second World War, when the government finally agreed that the place was at least worth preserving. However, that was as far as it went: an expression of patriotic sentiment but no action.

When the action came, it was from the idealistic, voluntary sector. A group of dedicated republicans, including the NGA, formed the Kilmainham Gaol Restoration Society. They focused – very wisely – on the primary ambition of restoring the fabric of the building, and determined on avoiding any references to the Civil War: the wounds were still too raw.

Kilmainham Gaol Restoration Society.

In 1960, the government handed the keys of Kilmainham to the society. A five-year lease was agreed, at the end of which ownership of the gaol would reside with the society provided that they restored the place to a condition fit for visitors. They demonstrated shrewd business acumen, raising funds by letting the place as a set for feature films.

The money was needed. Over 200,000 tons of debris had to be removed. Accomplishing that task alone required a huge commitment. By 1964, the roof was fixed. Along the way, the volunteers had gathered a series of exhibits and artefacts that would form the basis of the gaol's museum. The restored Kilmainham Gaol was officially opened in April 1966 by one of its most distinguished former inmates, Éamon de Valera, the 84-year-old President of Ireland.

Twenty years later, the restored gaol passed into the keeping of the OPW, a government agency. Previously, such agencies meant

A derelict staircase in the gaol.

delay and sclerosis. That didn't happen in this case: the OPW augmented the work of the volunteer groups to an even higher professional standard of restoration. It has overseen the transformation of Kilmainham Gaol into a museum that is one of the Irish capital's most popuar tourist and visitor attractions.

Looking up at the cells from the floor of the Victorian main hall of Kilmainham Gaol, which is now a museum.

A Major Tourist Attraction

It is worth summarising what the volunteers had achieved. When they started, the gaol had been neglected for nearly 40 years. Every window was broken; the gutters and all the timbering were rotten; there were weeds, ivy and every kind of vegetation everywhere. The place was infested with vermin.

After all the years of voluntary effort, the board of trustees returned the restored gaol to the care of the state in 1986. It is no exaggeration to say that the OPW has done a first-class job. It has curated the gaol with care, controlling the number of visitors at any one time and ensuring that only guided groups are permitted.

The potential for development as a visitor destination had always been there. As far back as 1938, a volunteer committee had received permission from Dublin County Council to hold an open day at the still unrestored prison. The response to the open day surprised everyone, exceeding even the most optimistic hopes. There was a constant queue of people waiting to gain entry, sometimes as much as a quarter of a mile long, from noon to 6pm. Yet despite this, and a later similar open day, it was clear that the full potential of the site would have to await its deserved restoration.

The prison as it is today, at sunset.

However, these open days were an indication of the place's attraction to visitors. Under the OPW's stewardship, Kilmainham – by now designated a national monument – has seen huge numbers of visitors, including, but not limited to Irish people interested in their country's past. It has also become one of Dublin's prime attractions for foreign visitors. Of all the sites under OPW management, it is second only to Dublin Castle in visitor numbers.

In 2017, the visitor figures amounted to an impressive 439,980 persons, of whom 431,340 were fully fee paying. (The others were concessions of one sort or another.) The gaol has also been part of a cultural and historical renewal of this part of the city, being now clustered with the nearby Irish Museum of Modern Art (IMMA) in the Royal Hospital and the Guinness Storehouse a little further away.

Of these, Kilmainham Gaol is the longest established visitor attraction and serves as a hub for visitors who are described as culturally curious. Not only do such visitors see the gaol itself and the museum, they get to visit a corner of Dublin – a little off the traditional beaten track – that previously did not attract many people. This has brought more business to local pubs and restaurants and performing arts spaces.

The whole story of the restoration is a matter for pride. It was a tremendous undertaking, brilliantly accomplished and consolidated. Comhghairdeas.

1st Visit to Kilmainham Voluntary Workers May 1960.

Select Bibliography

Jackson, Alvin, *Home Rule: An Irish History, 1800-2000,* London, Weidenfeld & Nicolson 2003

McGee, Owen, *The IRB: The Irish Republican Brotherhood from the Land League to Sinn Féin,* Dublin, Four Courts Press 2005

O Broin, Leon, *Revolutionary Underground: The Story of the Irish Republican Brotherhood, 1858-1924,* Totowa NJ, Rowman & Littlefield 1976

Stephens, James, *The Insurrection in Dublin,* Gerrards Cross, Colin Smythe 1992

Townshend, Charles, *Easter 1916: The Irish Rebellic* London, Allen Lane 2005

Townshend, Charles, *The Republic: The Fight for Iri Independence, 1918-1923,* London, Allen Lane 2013

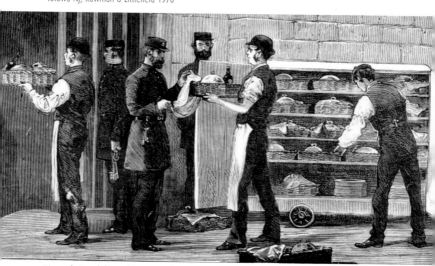

Dinner being delivered to upper class prisoners at Kilmainham, 19th century engraving.

Picture Credits

The publisher gratefully acknowledges the following image copyright holders. All images are copyright © individual rights holders unless stated otherwise. Every effort has been made to trace copyright holders, or copyright holders not mentioned here. If there have been any errors or omissions, the publisher would be happy to rectify this in any reprint.

1 Marc Lechanteur, S/Stock
3 Derick Hudson, S/Stock
4 Daniela Pace, S/Stock
5 Teapot Press
6 Teapot Press
13 Wiki Creative Commons
15 David Soanes, S/Stock
17 Wiki Creative Commons
18 Teapot Press
21 Teapot Press
22 Teapot Press
23 Teapot Press
24 Wiki Creative Commons
25 Peter Krocka, S/Stock
27 National Gallery of Ireland
28 Google Art Project
29 Lembi, S/Stock
30 Wiki Creative Commons
31 Wiki Creative Commons
32 Wiki Creative Commons
33 Historical Images Archive, Alamy
34 Vincent MacNamara, S/Stock
35 Peter Horree, Alamy
37 B O'Kane, Alamy
39 Florilegius, Alamy
40 Artokoloro, Alamy
42 National Portrait Gallery, London
43 The Print Collector, Alamy
45 Niday Picture Library, Alamy
46 Chris Bull, Alamy
47 Matthi, S/Stock
49 Album, Alamy
50 Wiki, Ulster Museum
51 Wiki Creative Commons
52 Wiki Creative Commons, (coloured)
53 Teapot Press, Bob Moulder
55 Wiki Creative Commons
56 Teapot Press
58 Wiki Creative Commons
59 Teapot Press
61 Wiki Creative Commons
61 Wiki Creative Commons
62 Teapot Press
63 Teapot Press
64 Wiki Creative Commons
65 Barry Mason, Alamy
66 Teapot Press
67 Wiki Creative Commons, (coloured)
69 Classic Image, Alamy
70 Library of Congress, (coloured)
71 Photo 12, Alamy
72 Library of Congress
73 Teapot Press
74 Wiki Creative Commons
75 Derick Hudson, S/Stock
77 Jackie Ellis, Alamy
78 Teapot Press
80 Pictorial Press Ltd, Alamy
81 Library of Congress
83 Teapot Press
85 Lebrecht Music & Arts, Alamy
87 Wiki Creative Commons, Meadows
89 19th Era, Alamy
90 Teapot Press
91 Wiki Creative Commons
92 Wiki Creative Commons
93 Wiki Creative Commons
95 Chronicle, Alamy
97 Library of Congress
99 Welcome Institute, CC 4.0
101 Illustrated London News
102 Illustrated London News
103 Teapot Press
104 The Granger Collection, Alamy
105 National Gallery of Ireland
106 Teapot Press
107 Wiki Creative Commons, (coloured)
108 Fabian Junge, S/Stock
109 Library of Congress
110 Wiki Creative Commons
111 Teapot Press
112 Wiki Creative Commons
113 Jerrye & Roy Klotz MD, Wiki Creative Commons
115 Library of Congress
116 Wiki Creative Commons, Clare LIbrary
117 Library of Congress
119 Willey Reveley
120 S/Stock, Lensfield
122 Library of Congress
123 Wiki Creative Commons
124 Teapot Press
125 Wiki Creative Commons
127 National Gallery of Ireland
128 Wiki Creative Commons, (coloured)
129 Teapot Press
131 Teapot Press
132 Library of Congress
134 Library of Congress
135 Teapot Press
137 Classic Image, Alamy
138 Wiki Creative Commons
138 Teapot Press
139 Teapot Press
140 Artokoloro, Alamy
141 Wiki Creative Commons
142 Teapot Press
143 Teapot Press, Vanity Fair
145 Pictorial Press Ltd, Alamy
146 Lanmas, Alamy
147 Lanmas, Alamy

Abbreviation: S/Stock: Shutterstock.

148 Teapot Press
149 Teapot Press
151 Teapot Press
153 Colin Waters, Alamy
155 Teapot Press
157 Courtesy of Kilmainham Gaol Museum/OPW, KMGLM.10PC-1B14-11
159 Library of Congress
160 S/Stock, Lensfield
162 Wiki Creative Commons, (coloured)
163 Teapot Press
164 National Library of Ireland on The Commons @ Flickr
166 Wiki Creative Commons, (coloured)
167 Wiki Creative Commons
168 Ray Morgan, S/Stock
168 Wiki Creative Commons
169 National Library of Ireland on The Commons @ Flickr
171 Wiki Creative Commons, (coloured)
172 Teapot Press
173 Wiki Creative Commons, (coloured)
174 Wiki Creative Commons, (coloured)
175 Wiki Creative Commons
176 Teapot Press
177 Wiki Creative Commons
177 D B Images, Alamy
178 Wiki Creative Commons, (coloured)
179 National Library of Ireland on The Commons @ Flickr
180 T W Murphy
181 Wiki Creative Commons

182 Wiki Creative Commons, (coloured)
184 Wiki Creative Commons, (coloured)
185 Wiki Creative Commons
186 Wiki Creative Commons, (coloured)
187 DMC Photography, Alamy
188 J.Hogan, S/Stock
189 Teapot Press
190 Wiki Creative Commons, (coloured)
191 Wiki Creative Commons, (coloured)
192 National Library of Ireland on The Commons @ Flickr
193 Chris Dorney, S/Stock
194 Wiki Creative Commons, (coloured)
195 Teapot Press
196 Wiki Creative Commons
197 Bureau of Military Archives
198 Wiki Creative Commons, (coloured)
200 National Library of Ireland on The Commons @ Flickr
201 Teapot Press
202 Wiki Creative Commons, (coloured)
204 Derick Hudson, S/Stock
205 Wiki Creative Commons
206 Wiki Creative Commons, (coloured)
207 National Gallery of Ireland
208 National Library of Ireland on The Commons @ Flickr
209 Teapot Press
210 Wiki Creative Commons
211 National Library of Ireland on The Commons @ Flickr

212 Wiki Creative Commons
213 Wiki Creative Commons
214 Wiki Creative Commons, (coloured)
216 Wiki Creative Commons
217 Teapot Press
218 National Library of Ireland on The Commons @ Flickr
219 National Library of Ireland on The Commons @ Flickr / manipulated
220 National Library of Ireland on The Commons @ Flickr / manipulated
222 Library of Congress, (coloured)
223 Wiki Creative Commons
224 Wiki Creative Commons
225 Wiki Creative Commons
226 National Gallery of Ireland
227 National Library of Ireland on The Commons @ Flickr / manipulated
228 Library of Congress
229 Teapot Press
230 Wiki Creative Commons, (coloured)
231 Unknown
232 Wiki Creative Commons
233 Courtesy of Kilmainham Gaol Museum/OPW, KMGLM.21PC-3K11-01
233 Wiki Creative Commons
234 Teapot Press
235 World History Archive, Alamy
237 National Library of Ireland on The Commons @ Flickr
238 National Library of Ireland on The Commons @ Flickr

239 Wiki Creative Commons, (coloured)
240 Phil Crean, Alamy
241 Vintage Space, Alamy
242 Wiki Creative Commons, (coloured)
245 kilmainham-inchicore.ie
246 Unknown
247 Kilmainham Gaol Restoration Society
248 Wiki Creative Commons
249 Salvador Maniquiz, S/Stock
251 P Gaborphotos, S/Stock
253 PA Images, Alamy
254 Teapot Press
     COVER IMAGES
     Library of Congress
     Teapot Press
     Fabian Junge / S/Stock
     Wiki Creative Commons
     Daniela Pace, S/Stock
     Wiki Creative Commons
     Teapot Press
     19th Era, Alamy
     Matthi, S/Stock
     Peter Horree, Alamy
     David Soanes, S/Stock
     Wiki Creative Commons
     Chris Bull, Alamy
     Lebrecht Music & Arts, Alamy
     Wiki Creative Commons
     Library of Congress
     Wiki Creative Commons
     National Portrait Gallery, London
     Wiki Creative Commons, colour enhanced

Abbreviation: S/Stock: Shutterstock.